The Don Carlos Enigma:
Variations of Historical Fictions

Maria-Cristina Necula

The Don Carlos Enigma:
Variations of Historical Fictions

Maria-Cristina Necula

Academica Press
Washington – London

Library of Congress Cataloging-in-Publication Data
Names: Necula, Maria-Cristina, author. |
Title: The don carlos enigma : variations of historical fictions / Maria-Cristina Necula
Description: Washington : Academica Press, 2020. | Includes references.
Identifiers: LCCN 2020938774 | ISBN 9781680539523 (hardcover)
ISBN 9781680538557 (paperback) ISBN 9781680538564 (ebook)
Copyright 2020 Maria-Cristina Necula

CONTENTS

ACKNOWLEDGMENTS vii

PREFACE ix

CHAPTER 1
History or the Origin of a Myth 1

CHAPTER 2
César Vichard de Saint-Réal:
Dom Carlos, nouvelle historique "Ce malheureux héritier" 19

CHAPTER 3
Friedrich Schiller:
Don Karlos, Infant von Spanien "Nenne mich Du" 51

CHAPTER 4
Giuseppe Verdi: *Don Carlos* "In un mondo migliore" 81

CHAPTER 5
The Sound of Words 109

APPENDIX 125
Interview with Ramón Vargas 125
Entrevista con Ramón Vargas 129
Interview with Kamal Khan 133
José Cura on *Don Carlos* 135

BIBLIOGRAPHY 137

INDEX 145

ACKNOWLEDGMENTS

I would like to express my profound gratitude to André Aciman for his inspiring guidance, insightful feedback, and constant support throughout my work on this project while I was a doctoral student. This study would not have come into existence without him. His unceasing encouragement to be bold in following my own writing voice has given me wings not only as a writer, but also as a human being. And thanks to him, I will forever cherish that treasure trove of wisdom, history, and understanding of human nature named Saint-Réal.

Many thanks go to Paolo Fasoli for his helpful and knowledgeable comments on libretti and operatic history, and Marvin Carlson for reacquainting me with the world of theatre and for his expertise on Schiller.

I remain indebted to opera stars José Cura and Ramón Vargas, and to pianist/conductor extraordinaire, Kamal Khan, for their feedback and for their participation in Chapter Five.

To Paul du Quenoy at Academica Press: my jubilant thanks for your enthusiasm and support in offering a home to this journey of variations on the history of Don Carlos.

My deepest admiration goes to the three Masters who have attempted to solve the Don Carlos enigma, each through his own enthralling interpretation of history, César Vichard de Saint-Réal, Friedrich Schiller, and Giuseppe Verdi: spending time in your literary and musical company has offered me some of the richest, most enlightening intellectual and emotional experiences of my entire life. May humanity continue to discover and rediscover you eternally.

Finally, I wish to convey my love and infinite thankfulness to my parents. The completion of this book as well as the achievement of all the milestones in my life would not have been possible without their unwavering love and belief in me.

PREFACE

The history of the sixteenth-century Spanish prince, Don Carlos, has inspired writers and composers of Spain, France, England, Germany, and Italy into producing creative treatments that, despite the artistic limitations of historically-based origins, demonstrate an extraordinary range of imaginative freedom. The first-known literary treatment was the play *El Principe Don Carlos* by Don Diego Ximénez de Enciso—premiered in 1622 and published in 1634. Yet the practice of taking creative liberties with the story of Don Carlos began long before, as fictional invention sprouted from within actual historical accounts. The seeds of the myth created around the prince were planted in European consciousness as early as 1568, during the last months of his life. Imprisoned by orders of his father, King Philip II, he died during his incarceration, and to this day, the actual cause of death remains unknown. The official explanation for the Spanish Infante's incarceration was that he had become a political threat due to his mental instability, and that his death was self-induced by erratic behavior. Yet various accounts recorded in political reports and in historical works insinuated that he had been murdered by orders of his father. At the same time, Philip's brutal suppression of the revolt in the Netherlands was enflaming an already-simmering widespread hatred of Spain. Flemish nobles who had escaped to Germany launched an anti-Spanish propaganda that, through the use of pamphlets and word-of-mouth rumors, contributed to constructing the

"Black Legend" around the Spanish nation and King Philip. The propagandists seized on Don Carlos's mysterious death as propitious content for their mission. Their foray into speculative fiction was supported by various diplomatic statements, particularly from the Venetian and English ambassadors who had been at court during the disappearance of the Infante, and who insinuated foul play.

Such immediate sliding into fiction under the guise of history reveals a remarkable fluidity between history and fiction that, while pertinent to innumerable portrayals of historical personages of other eras and nationalities, seems to acquire a particularly transformational narrative power in the case of Don Carlos. On one hand, this subject bears the gravity of historical validity, and, on the other, the unsettled nature of its historical content invites interpretation while stimulating innovation within the genre that houses the interpretation. Discernible advancements within genres did not occur in most of the creative versions of the Don Carlos story. But the three treatments on which the fluidity and transformational impetus at the intersection of history and fiction had a highly potent impact are César de Saint-Réal's novel, *Dom Carlos, nouvelle historique* (1672), Friedrich Schiller's play, *Don Karlos, Infant von Spanien* (1787), and Giuseppe Verdi's opera, *Don Carlos* (1867).

This book is concerned with exploring the elements of innovation that Saint-Réal, Schiller, and Verdi contributed to their genres in their treatments of the Don Carlos story. While considering the network of historical, political, cultural, economic, and biographical factors that impacted the creation of their works, I will reflect on how the particular blend of history and fiction around the personage of Don Carlos inspired the two authors and the composer to take creative liberties. Within each of their treatments, I will identify certain pivotal points of narrative, semantic, dramatic, and musical transformation that served them in instituting these liberties and transcending conventions of their genres. All of these pivotal points are anchored in history: either in historically-documented actions or, on a more abstract level, in historically-based principles and forces that arrive at confrontation. The fluid history of Don Carlos thus animates the core of this mechanism of transformation by offering at once historical authority and mystery, and fostering a fertile arena for different manifestations of historical fiction.

The book is divided into five chapters, and organized around highlighting the pivotal points of transformation by focusing on plot and close readings of selected scenes while drawing on critical, historical, biographical studies in the fields of seventeenth-century French literature, eighteenth-century German theatre, nineteenth-century French and Italian opera, Spanish history, politics, philosophical treatises, and other relevant artistic works. Chapter One presents an overview of sixteenth-century Spanish history and situates the principal personages, Don Carlos, Philip, and Elisabeth as well as their actions within a documented historical context. Chapters Two, Three, and Four are each devoted to the treatment of the Don Carlos story by Saint-Réal, Schiller, and Verdi, respectively, contextualizing them within their epochs, cultural milieus, and several of their other œuvres. Chapter Five adds an additional dimension to the process of recreating Don Carlos: operatic performance, in which the complex partnership of vocal music and text provides a unique opportunity to recast the character in a continuously-evolving mold representative of its fluid, open-ended historical origins.

CHAPTER 1

History or the Origin of a Myth

"Believe me, Your Majesty, if this were not true, I would not write it to you," wrote Prince Philip, Regent of Spain, to his father, Holy Roman Emperor Charles V, in March 1545, describing the terrible financial situation in certain Spanish provinces. This appears to be an early representative phrase of the one who would become King Philip II, also known as Felipe el Prudente—Philip the Prudent. His directness, succinctness, and appreciation of truth and facts along with his courteousness and self-mastery would make him an indomitable, albeit cautious, ruler. During Philip's thirty-two-year reign (January 1556 – September 1598), Spain would experience its Golden Age, owning territories on almost every continent, and exerting its geographical, political, and economic dominance as "the empire on which the sun never sets." Yet there is another self-descriptive quote that would come to reflect the public perception of Philip's personality: "'I don't know if they think I'm made of iron or stone. The truth is, they need to see that I am mortal, like everyone else.'" His desire to maintain peace at all costs, his personal tragedies, his stoicism, his refusal to defend himself against international accusations and propaganda, and his impossible responsibility of keeping the burdening inheritance of the Netherlands under control contributed to create the despotic and taciturn public image, so different, in many respects, from the private Philip. To this image was added the mystery and speculation around the death of his son and heir, Don Carlos, which imbued the father-son relationship with a fictional aura, even within contemporary historical accounts and political reports. This created an inextricable connection between history and fiction that would inspire numerous authors in their interpretations of the Don Carlos story whose dramatic core lies in the enigmatic relationship between father and son.

Sixteenth-century Spain was formed of provinces ruled by the local nobility, and while the king governed all of them, he did not have complete authority over them. Although culturally unrefined compared to other European monarchies, with a majority of the population being illiterate, Spain was receptive to cultural influences from Italy and the Netherlands, and its aristocrats traveled to Italy for education. The royal court was not very sophisticated, yet the Italian humanist Castiglione settled in Spain and wrote his famous book, *The Courtier*, while living there. Spanish troops stationed in Germany and Flanders to protect the empire against the Ottoman threat contributed to creating a general negative opinion abroad and aroused hostility towards everything related to Spain. This hostility was also fueled by lack of knowledge about the Spanish and by the unfavorable reports presented by Venetian ambassadors who frequently spent time in the monarchy. But inside the country the intolerance and cruelty that the Spanish were known for had diminished considerably since the 1520s. During Philip's reign the *conversos*—Christians of Jewish origin—were no longer persecuted but accepted into public life. Even Philip's personal secretary, Gonzalo Pérez, was of *converso* origin and a humanist.

Appointed Regent of Spain in 1543, at sixteen years of age, Philip maintained a constant, direct correspondence with his frequently-absent father, keeping him informed about state matters. Unafraid to refuse the emperor financial aid for his war campaigns, the future inheritor of the Spanish crown demonstrated, from the beginning, mature, independent thinking and fairness in protecting the population of Spain and the Netherlands from over-taxation. While he seemed mildly aggravated at these refusals, the emperor manifested great tolerance and appreciated his son's assertiveness. To this self-reliance was added the fact that, from an early age, Philip was instilled with the belief that his actions were divinely sanctioned. His attentive involvement in council meetings and his consideration of all council members' advices before making a decision, his non-participation at executions, his preference for preserving prosperity by peace rather than increasing it by war paint a very different picture from the tyrant of the novelistic, theatrical, and operatic treatments of his character. His penchant for court festivities, music, chivalry literature and rites, large-scale jousting tournaments, dancing, entertaining, hunting, and gallantries with women, his studies of Erasmus and humanism, and his appreciation of Flemish culture and art depict an open-minded personality full of life and curiosity about the world. In fact, except for Charles, Philip became the most-traveled monarch of his time: half of the first sixteen years of his reign were spent touring Western Europe with his father, visiting the territories that belonged to Spain in order to be recognized as heir to them. Philip's only social hindrances were his inexperience with sophisticated court protocols and his lack of talent for languages: he spoke only Spanish fluently, was proficient in Portuguese, and knew some Latin. Initially, he gave the impression that he was rigid due to his awkwardness with formalities, and taciturn because he could not participate in conversations with those who did not speak his native language. Yet he always left a most favorable impression on court ladies, regardless of their nationality, as he was extremely chivalrous and attentive to them. He also earned admiration for his hunting, dancing, and sports abilities. On the European tour he jousted with that ill-starred, brave personage whom he later allowed to be executed by the Duke of Alba to enforce the suppression of the Dutch Revolt: Lamoral, Count of Egmont, governor of Flanders and Artois.

As a child Philip had been very close to his mother, Isabel of Portugal, but lost her when he was twelve. He venerated his father and suffered greatly during the latter's long campaigns, compensating for the absence of loving parents by developing unusually close bonds to his two younger sisters, Maria and Juana. Nevertheless, the most significant relationship for Philip was the one with his father. He absorbed as much as possible from Charles V and continued to revere the emperor after his death, never uttering any hint of criticism against him. It was the emperor who, first-hand, instructed Philip on how to rule and gave him wise insights on the people at court. One such insight was about the Duke of Alba's excessive ambition: "'You are younger than he; take care that he does not dominate you. Be careful not to let him or the other grandees get a firm footing in government.'" Twenty years older than Philip, the Duke of Alba instructed Philip in warfare and became the center of influence of one of the two groups into which Philip's closest courtiers were divided. The other group was led by Ruy Gómez, Prince of Eboli, who became very close to the King, and was sometimes referred to as "Rey" (king) Gómez for his power. Philip allowed for conflicting views and policies to develop among his courtiers and managed to keep everyone's unwavering devotion. As high steward to the King, the Duke of Alba was unsatisfied with his role and wanted an even higher position in the monarchy but, while Philip often consulted him on Flanders, he did not promote him. Philip's distrust of Alba, as will be illustrated in Schiller's *Don Karlos*, was not overt but influenced him nevertheless. Ruy Gómez enjoyed Philip's favor until he began to support Egmont and William of Orange in their pleas for religious freedom in the Netherlands; then, he was removed from his central role in politics and assigned to Don Carlos and his household.

Philip's matrimonial union with Elisabeth de Valois—who was initially betrothed to his son, the Infante Don Carlos—was a happy one. It was his third and best marriage thus far, after the two-year loveless marital relationship with María of Portugal—Don Carlos's mother who died four days after giving birth to him—and the strictly political four-year marriage to England's Mary Tudor, who was eleven years his senior. The King was known for having many lovers but when he married Elisabeth, it was reported that the newlyweds were very "pleased with each other," and Ruy Gómez notified the French ambassador that Philip's "'past love affairs have ceased, and everything is going so well that one could not wish for more.'"

When Elisabeth was sent to France, her mother, Catherine de Medici, entrusted her with the political mission to secure a marriage between Don Carlos and her sister, Marguerite de Valois, who would later become Henry IV's wife. The new Spanish Queen immediately endeared herself to the Infante, especially by manifesting compassion for him during his frequent fever attacks. There was no love story between Elisabeth and Don Carlos. Their closeness stemmed from the French-born Spanish Queen's political agenda. An additional marriage between Spanish and

French royalty would have made the alliance between Spain and France indestructible. But Philip was against forming yet another bond to Catherine de Medici. He preferred Mary Stuart as a wife for his son in order to bring England under his control. The prospect of this marriage failed not only because of Elisabeth and Catherine's machinations against it, but also because Philip, aware of his son's worsening mental condition, procrastinated until it was too late and Mary Stuart married her cousin, Henry Stuart, Lord Darnley. Don Carlos's alarming mental and physical condition was recorded in various accounts; one such diplomatic report attests to the nationwide concern about the Infante's abilities as the future inheritor of the Spanish crown: "'he walks hunched over and seems weak on his legs,' but is 'much given to violence to the point of cruelty… He has abandoned himself to such chaos that… the joy among the Spaniards at having a native prince is as great as the doubts they have about his ability to govern.'"

The extensive inbreeding among his royal relatives was certainly responsible for Don Carlos's mental and physical defects. Philip was the child of first cousins, both grandchildren of Ferdinand and Isabella. Philip's mother, Queen Isabella, came from several generations of consanguineous unions. In 1564, Imperial ambassador Adam von Dietrichstein described the nineteen-year old Don Carlos in a letter to the emperor: "'brown, curly hair, long in the jaw, pale of face… One of his shoulders is slightly higher than the other. He has a sunken chest, and a little lump on his back at waist height. His left leg is much longer than his right… he has weak legs. His voice is harsh and sharp, he has problems in speaking and the words come with difficulty from his mouth.'"

Reports of the Infante's sadistic and violent nature had spread throughout the main European courts. It was said that he enjoyed seeing animals roasted alive, and whipping servants and young girls. He rode one of his father's best horses with such violence that the horse died. He once bit off the head of a turtle that had bitten his finger. From the very little time that Charles V spent with his grandson, the former emperor commented that he disliked the boy's personality and was concerned about his future. Don Carlos was often debilitated by bouts of quartan fever, a malarial fever recurring at three-day intervals. His mental condition was worsened by the accident he suffered at the University of Alcalá in 1561. While chasing a girl, he fell down a flight of stairs and smashed his head into a door. His wound developed into an infection that nearly killed him. The trepanation procedure performed on him by the famous doctor Andreas Vesalius proved less successful than religious superstition. After the remains of local priest Diego de Alcalá, considered to have healing properties, were brought to the Infante's bed, the latter began to recover within hours of having touched the mummified body and passed his hands across his face. In five weeks Don Carlos recuperated but the entire experience increased his violent rages.

The Spanish prince's physical and mental defects were the consequences not only of the in-breeding within his family but also of a horrendously difficult birth. This was followed by a childhood deprived of parental love—Don Carlos never knew his mother and his father was frequently absent—and the affectionate bonds he developed were constantly cut short. At eleven months he experienced the loss of his wet nurse, and at age seven he was abruptly separated from both his aunt Juana and his governess to whom he felt very close. His emotionally-starved childhood combined with the physical and mental challenges he experienced most likely contributed to creating a personality at once prone to violent rages and demanding of affection and devotion from anyone who showed him any hint of compassion. Often, he behaved like a child, asking questions indiscriminately and persistently, and openly manifesting his displeasure, even in council meetings, at the slightest detail that did not fulfill his expectations. At times, however, Don Carlos demonstrated great generosity towards women, especially towards Elisabeth, and regaled them with expensive gifts.

Philip tried his utmost to treat his son as normal, hoping that with age, his condition might improve and he would be capable of ruling. In spite of his defects, Don Carlos was, in several accounts, described as intelligent and astute. His father attempted to include him in governmental matters by allowing him to participate in the Council of State meetings. In his testament of 1557, Philip had named Don Carlos his official heir, and in 1559, during his speech to the States of the Netherlands, he declared that he would appoint Don Carlos as governor of the Low Countries. He even arranged a marriage for his son with Anna of Austria, the daughter of his cousin Emperor Maximilian II, but eventually, increasingly concerned about his son's mental state, he evaded the attempts to move forward with the wedding plans. The general impression that had formed about the Spanish prince was that he led a kind of double life oscillating between normality and insanity. At the same time, Philip's move of Ruy Gómez to the Infante's household backfired as Gómez tried to persuade Don Carlos to support the interests of his faction which included advocating for the Netherlands. Influenced by Gómez, Don Carlos's delusions developed to alarming proportions. When Egmont came to Madrid, the Infante wanted to establish ties with him, while the former became interested in Ruy Gómez' "strange prince of peace." Consequently, when the Duke of Alba was appointed as governor of the Netherlands instead of him, Don Carlos became infuriated not only that Philip had broken his promise but also that his rights and capabilities were not being recognized. At first, he threatened to kill Alba, and then his murderous rage turned on his father as Philip had promised to take him, along with John of Austria, to the Netherlands himself, but then cancelled the voyage.

The Netherlands were of both economic and sentimental importance to Spain: eighty percent of the trade routes that Spain used were from the Netherlands, major loans for financing the emperor's military campaigns were negotiated and supported by the Netherlands, and most of the Castilian wool was sold there. Not to mention that Philip's father was born in Ghent, and his grandfather in Bruges. However, the creation of the Low Countries as Charles V envisioned it was an imperialist artifice. The emperor had added Flanders and Artois to the former Imperial domains in which Dutch and German were spoken and had named himself Lord of the Netherlands. Each province sent representatives to the States General, the parliament of the Low Countries, but the lack of political unity between them simmered under the surface. Charles V was, to a great extent, responsible not only for this sentiment of disunity in the Low Countries but also for the hostility they felt towards Spain, particularly due to religious imposition without forewarning. Philip reinforced Charles V's policies and had Spanish troops—called *tercios*—stationed throughout the Netherlands. He appointed his half-sister, Margaret of Parma, as the Regent in Brussels, and demanded that anti-heresy laws be strictly enforced, which the leading nobles of the Netherlands refused to do. Margaret constantly negotiated between the Dutch nobility's pleas for religious tolerance and enforcement of Philip's decrees. In December 1564, William of Orange addressed the Brussels council and advocated for "liberty of conscience." In 1565, the Count of Egmont arrived in Spain to present the Netherlands' grievances and requests directly to the King. While Philip gave Egmont the impression of yielding to his demands and adopting a more tolerant attitude towards the Protestants in the Netherlands and their right to worship, he actually ordered Margaret to continue enforcing his policies and show no clemency towards anyone suspected of heresy. The introduction of the Inquisition in the Netherlands was the most incendiary issue that incited the Dutch nobility to rebellion. It remains a contested issue between historians: some attribute it directly to Philip's decrees, while others claim that Philip never wanted to bring the Inquisition into the Netherlands and that much of the religious oppression resulted from the actions of Cardinal de Granvelle, chief councilor to Margaret, who interpreted and enacted Philip's repressive policies towards heretics. It was rather Philip's support of the local religious powers that was interpreted by the Dutch nobility as leading to an imposition of the Inquisition. Philip is said to have denied his intention to introduce the Inquisition directly to the Flemish ambassador, Baron Montigny, as early as 1562: "'Never in my imagination… have I thought of introducing into Flanders the Inquisition of Spain.'" However, as with Egmont, he was, most likely, misleading the baron. In truth, Philip believed in nipping heresy in the bud in order to maintain stability in his realm and viewed the Inquisition as his most effective instrument in eliminating any trace of religious dissent. He was concerned that any compromise with the Dutch nobles would lead to a situation of war as in France where the Wars of Religion between Catholics and Calvinist Protestants—Huguenots—had begun in 1562 and would last until 1598. As the situation in Flanders worsened—Catholic churches were being desecrated and priests killed—Philip decided to send an army to suppress the rebellion and chose the Duke of Alba as its commander and new governor of the Netherlands. In the spring of 1566, Alba and his troops departed on their mission, which was the last straw in Don Carlos's determination to rebel against his father.

The Infante entreated John of Austria to help him assert his right and take the position of governor from Alba. He wrote to the grandees—nobles—for support and planned his escape from Spain to the Netherlands. John reported everything to Philip. Don Carlos's plan to flee to the Low Countries forced the King to restrict the former's irrational actions that could only be damaging to a monarchy already in the ferment of suppressing rebellious forces. Before midnight on 18 January 1568, Philip, dressed in armor and accompanied by four Council of State members, including Ruy Gómez, and four assistants, went to the Infante's bedroom, took all his papers and weapons, and ordered the windows boarded up. Don Carlos is reported to have asked: "'Has your Majesty come to kill me?'" to which Philip responded in the negative and added that "he would now treat him not as a father ought to but as a king should." The Infante tried to throw himself into the fire. When a guard restrained him, he cried to his father: "'Does your Majesty want to tie me down like a madman? I am not mad, just desperate'" to which Philip replied: "'Calm yourself, prince, and get into bed. What we are doing is for your own good.'" No one would be permitted to have contact with Don Carlos, except for the six courtiers guarding him. Upon hearing the news of the Infante's incarceration, Elisabeth wept for days. The entire court and country were in shock, and Philip spent the next days meeting with his various councils to explain that he had acted for the benefit of the kingdom. He promised to provide more details in the future, and he forbid any further discussion on the matter as well as any mention of Don Carlos in the sermons of priests. At first, the general impression throughout European courts was that Philip was only punishing his son. But the King made it clear that Don Carlos's imprisonment would not be temporary. Justifying the Infante's incarceration, Philip wrote to the Infante's grandmother—dowager queen of Portugal, Catherine, who was the only surviving sister of Charles V therefore Philip's aunt; her daughter, Maria, had been Philip's first wife and first cousin—"'the prince's condition has deteriorated so far and reached such a state that, in order to discharge the obligation that as a Christian prince I have towards God and towards the kingdoms and dominions that He has chosen to place in my charge, I could not avoid making a change to his situation, arresting and imprisoning him... My decision does not derive from any crime, disobedience or disrespect, nor does it aim to punish because although there was plenty of evidence for that it could have waited the proper time and place. Nor is this a means to an end, hoping... in this way to reform his excesses and disorders. The problem has another root and origin that neither time nor treatment can solve.'" He explained that his paternal love had not been enough and he had been unable to find any cure for his son. To Catherine de Medici, Don Carlos's maternal grandmother, Philip wrote: "I never hope to see my son restored to his right mind again. I have chosen in this matter to make a sacrifice to God of my own flesh and blood, preferring His service and the universal good to all other human considerations." To the Pope, he explained that his actions were caused by Don Carlos's inability to rule because of his mental derangements and physical deformities, and not because he was a heretic or a rebel: the Infante had become a matter of state security, a real threat to the stability of the monarchy. There is said to have been a secret trial of Don Carlos before the Grand Inquisitor, Cardinal Espinosa, among others, during which the Infante's defiance and disobedience served as the main reasons to charge him with treason, but documentation about this trial was never discovered. Philip protested against the rumors that his son was conspiring against him, and insisted that Don Carlos was not a heretic. He organized a series of public investigations into the Infante's behavior, some of which he attended. Ruy Gómez told the French ambassador, Fourquevaux, that Philip had already been aware for a few years that Don Carlos was mentally ill, and that he had waited, in vain, for signs of improvement.

During the six months of his incarceration, the Infante behaved erratically, alternating between starving himself and over-eating, swallowing his diamond ring in the hope that it was poisonous, and ordering ice to sleep on. At last he succeeded in inducing his annihilation; he caught a fever and died on 24 July. He was buried in Madrid in the church of St. Domingo and his body was transferred to the Escorial in 1573. Antonio Pérez, replacing his father as secretary to the King, reported that Philip wept for three days, and the court went into a year of mourning. The King entered a period of depression that would be compounded by yet another loss. On 3 October, Elisabeth died in giving a premature birth to a stillborn girl. The double tragedy of losing both his son—and only successor to the throne—and his wife within three months affected Philip profoundly but he bore his grief stoically and kept it very private: "'…I accept to the best of my ability the divine will which ordains as it pleases.'" But in the public perception, both in Spain and throughout Europe, the two deaths occurring within such a short period of time fueled rumors about foul play that, combined with Philip's tyrannical suppression of the Flemish rebellion, would become ammunition for the already-growing anti-Spain propaganda.

As the Duke of Alba's army of 10,000 troops was approaching Brussels, two Spanish Protestants published the *Art of the Holy Spanish Inquisition*. The account instilled such terror that the nobles restored order immediately, which compelled Margaret to ask Philip to stop Alba's advance. But it was too late. Alba arrived in Brussels on 22 August 1567. As soon as he settled in, he established a tribunal called the Council of Troubles, which would come to be known as the Council of Blood, and arrested the Count of Egmont along with other prominent nobles. William of Orange had already escaped to Germany in April 1567 while many of the Low Countries' inhabitants found refuge in either France or England. From Germany, William organized a series of attacks on Alba's troops, yet he did not have enough money to pay his hired army. Alba made a terrifying public example of Egmont and the Count of Horn by having them executed for treason in Brussels's public square on 5 June 1568. The executions sent ripples of outrage throughout European courts. For the following three years, the Duke instituted a reign of terror and persecution of anyone who showed the slightest sign of heresy or rebellion. The numbers are horrific: 9,000 were fined, imprisoned, or had their property seized; 1,700 were executed—this would be ten times as many as the Spanish Inquisition would execute throughout Philip's reign. As many as 60,000 fled the Netherlands in 1567 and 1568. Historians have suggested that Philip could have prevented this massacre had he gone to the Netherlands in person to settle matters. In fact, he was repeatedly advised to do so by his councilors in both Brussels and Spain. Although apparently willing to go, Philip procrastinated, and this gave the impression that he manifested indifference towards the Flemish nobility as towards his Spanish advisors, which only aggravated the conflict.

In the post-Reformation disunified Christian Europe, Spain, as the foremost proponent of Tridentine Orthodoxy, became, in the Protestants' view, a symbol of evil, oppression, and superstition. The already-fermenting European hostility towards the Spanish monarchy was intensified in the 1560s' by the revolt in the Low Countries. Combined with an international opinion of Philip as an imperialist along with a widespread envy and fear of Spanish power, it is not surprising that various sources seized on the imprisonment and mysterious death of Don Carlos to spread rumors about Philip's inhuman tyranny and launch an anti-Spain propaganda, thus contributing to creating the Spanish Black Legend—*La leyenda negra*. The myth created around Don Carlos and its obscuration of historical facts originate, in large part, from this anti-Spain propaganda.

French, Venetian, and British ambassadors had given various accounts testifying both to the Infante's mental instability and rages—which were justifiable reasons for Philip to shut him away—as to Philip's cruelty in not allowing anyone to visit his son, and possibly poisoning him. Some ambassadorial reports reported the death as a suicide. The only non-Catholic ambassador at the Spanish court at the time of the Infante's arrest, the English diplomat, John Man, changed his story for personal reasons. At first, he reported that Don Carlos was arrested because of his instability.

But when he was dismissed from the court, Man, in anger, began to spread the rumor of the Infante's possible poisoning on orders of his father. The ambassadorial reports were only the beginning. Elisabeth's death three months after Don Carlos fired up speculation and provided additional content to Philip's many enemies who rapidly spread their net of reputation-smearing. As the Duke of Alba's massacre in the Netherlands greatly amplified international outrage and hatred of Spain, it launched William of Orange's propaganda and precipitated the Dutch Revolt. Within forty years of Don Carlos's death, a series of published works, including historical compilations, succeeded in constructing the myth about the Infante's supposed murder and the Black Legend around Philip and his Spanish realm.

The first two published accounts of the anti-Spain, anti-Philip propaganda, that also proliferated the Don Carlos myth, appeared in the Netherlands in 1581. One was an anonymous work in verse, entitled *Diogenes*, in which the author asked the French king to help the Dutch combat Philip's oppressive rule, and planted the seeds of the forbidden love myth that would be exploited in so many adaptations of the Don Carlos story. The message in *Diogenes* was that Don Carlos and Elisabeth had both been murdered by Philip for falling in love. The better known account, William of Orange's *Apology*, claimed that Philip "'unnaturally murdered his own son and heir.'" It condemned the entire Spanish race for their cruelty and avarice as well as for treating the Low Countries inhabitants in the same manner as the colonized Indians in America. William accused Philip of being an incestuous bigamist, and a murderer, not only of Don Carlos but also of Elisabeth. The murder of Don Carlos remains the longest-lasting among all of William of Orange's accusations against Philip II. In 1587, French Protestant historian Louis Turquet de Mayerne published his colossal work on the history of Spain in twenty-seven volumes, *Histoire Générale d'Espagne*, in which he maintains this accusation. At the start of the seventeenth century, Pierre Matthieu wrote a fictional interpretation of the story in his *Histoire de France* (Paris, 1606) that ends in Don Carlos's execution by four slaves by order of the Inquisition. Historian Jacques Auguste de Thou also intimated foul play around Don Carlos's death in his historical accounts that became the monumental work, *Historia sui temporis*, published between 1604 and 1608.

What remains perplexing is Philip's unwillingness to defend himself against William of Orange's indictments, which increased the speculation that he had something to hide. Some theories assert that Philip simply refused to declare his son insane in front of the entire world to justify his actions, therefore he preferred to remain silent. It did not help that he did not allow anyone to write about his life and accomplishments during his lifetime, as he despised flattery. The courtier Luis Cabrera de Córdoba did keep chronicles on Philip's life and activities, and was considered the official court historiographer. His historical opus, *Historia de Felipe I, Rey de España*, published more than twenty years after Philip's death, is regarded as the best chronicle of the king's life. But Cabrera's depiction of the King rushing to the dying Don Carlos and making the sign of the cross over him is undoubtedly biased; he is the only one of Philip's contemporaries who mentions such a scene. It is worth noting that the anti-Spain propaganda was also aided by pamphlets and rumors of a conspiracy theory supported by forged decrees of the

Inquisition to demonstrate the intention of a mass annihilation of the Low Countries inhabitants.

Thus, the challenge to accuracy lies in the fact that even historical accounts may be as fictional as the literary, theatrical, and operatic treatments of the Don Carlos story. The more temperate historical approaches to relating what truly occurred implied that Philip had to imprison his son, both for the latter's and the monarchy's safety. Yet there are documented statements of a certain inflexibility in the King's behavior that have been used against him to paint him as cruel and capable of atrocious deeds. One of the best historians on Philip and Don Carlos, Louis Prosper Gachard, tried to remain objective and present all facets of Philip's personality including his tender, paternal behavior towards his daughters. Still he could not completely escape the almost three-century-old shadow of suspicion cast on Philip as the author of the Infante's death, whether directly or not.

And neither can historians today. The seeds of the Don Carlos myth are embedded into history. Fictional variations existed from the start in the historical accounts themselves, rendering the line between history and fiction almost invisible. Don Carlos's history itself seemed to extend the invitation to interpretation, an invitation that so many authors throughout the subsequent centuries have found irresistible. Yet few have succeeded in channeling the fluidity between history and fiction in a more genre-transformative manner than César Vichard de Saint-Réal, Friedrich Schiller, and Giuseppe Verdi.

CHAPTER 2

César Vichard de Saint-Réal: *Dom Carlos, nouvelle historique* "Ce malheureux héritier"*

The instant success of César Vichard de Saint-Réal's *Dom Carlos, nouvelle historique*, published in 1672, prompted a series of immediate responses, translations, and adaptations. In 1673, an anonymous work, *Sentiments d'un homme d'esprit sur la nouvelle intitulée "Dom Carlos,"* encouraged Saint-Réal to write a continuation of his novel that would include additional discussions about politics and love. That same year, *Dom Carlos* was translated into English and became the source of Thomas Otway's play *Don Carlos, Prince of Spain*, whose premiere took place in 1676 in London. The play was a commercial and financial triumph with an uncharacteristically long run of ten days. Nine years later, Jean-Galbert de Campistron's *Andronic* transplanted the Don Carlos story to antiquity. In the eighteenth century, French poet Augustin-Louis, marquis de Ximénès, and Italian dramatist, Count Vittorio Alfieri created their *Dom Carlos* (1761) and *Filippo II* (1783), respectively. After reading Saint-Réal's novel, Friedrich Schiller fundamentally transformed the interpretation of the story along with its dramaturgical structure in his *Don Karlos, Infant von Spanien* (1787).

---

* This unhappy inheritor (*Dom Carlos*, 137).

The nineteenth-century works based on the Don Carlos legend initially responded to both Saint-Réal and Schiller, but eventually focused on the latter. Marie-Joseph Chénier and Eugène Cormon conceived the never-staged *Philippe II* and the long-titled *Philippe II, roi d'Espagne, drame en cinq actes imité de Schiller, et précédé de l'Étudiant d'Alcalá prologue* (1846), respectively; these works, among others, reflected the waning of Saint-Réal's influence and the increase of Schiller's. *Don Karlos, Infant von Spanien* is, thus, a turning point for Saint-Réal's novel: nineteenth-century considerations of the story shifted focus to the German playwright and, for the most part, disregarded the Savoyard writer. It was Verdi's opera that, in 1867, returned the spotlight to the *nouvelle historique*: Saint-Réal's *Dom Carlos* was published in a new edition in France that year. The last-known dramatic interpretation dates from 1901: *Philippe II* by Belgian Symbolist poet, Emile Verhaeren. While attesting to the enduring influence of Saint-Réal's *nouvelle historique*, the numerous adaptations that followed Otway's play have obscured the fact that *Dom Carlos* is the first novelistic treatment of the Spanish prince's story. Interest in the novel, along with critical analyses and acknowledgments of its innovative merits, would remain largely dormant until the twentieth century.

A native of Chambéry, in the Duchy of Savoy, Saint-Réal was educated by the Jesuits in Lyon. In 1663, he moved to Paris where he found employment as an archivist at the royal library under the supervision of Antoine Varillas. It was a time of new developments in French literature. A year earlier, Madame de La Fayette's *La Princesse de Montpensier* had been published anonymously. This short novel would eventually be considered by some as the first *nouvelle historique*. Yet, throughout the seventeenth century that designation would remain flexible, incorporating elements of the *nouvelle galante*. Historical settings, personages, and details were mingled with love stories and fictional characters. Factual accuracy was often sacrificed in favor of exploring moral dilemmas. Madame de Villedieu's *Annales galantes* (1670) exemplified this fluidity of the *nouvelle historique*. Many novelists were inspired by the inclination to grant voices to characters that historians had kept silent. Their creative liberties set the stage for an increased literary interest in the analysis of individuals' psychological motivations that would blossom into the *roman d'analyse* with Madame de La Fayette's *La Princesse de Clèves* (1678). The proclivity towards analysis also stemmed from a general preoccupation with reason and the intellectualization of emotions, not limited to literature. In the *tragèdies lyriques* as in philosophy and salon debates, passion, desire, and sexual love were similarly viewed as weaknesses that led to defeat and to the loss of personal freedom, reputation, and glory. The noblest aim was to remain in control of one's own heart and to defer the surrender to passion for as long as possible. Descartes's *Les passions de l'âme* (1649) influenced rational theories about human emotions for the next century and a half, while in salon conversations, les Précieuses analyzed issues of love and morality as well as the refinement of passionate conduct and expression. It is very probable that, not long after his arrival in Paris, Saint-Réal attended the conversations between Antoine Varillas and Gilles Ménage who was known as the "oracle of the Précieuses." He also met Racine, Boileau, La Fontaine, and Molière. The cultural and social influences of the Parisian metropolis immersed the Savoyard into a complex milieu where he would come to know instant success followed by disappointment.

Before writing his first *nouvelle historique* Saint-Réal manifested a political agenda determined by financial considerations rather than by his own convictions, with a work of prose and verse, *Réconciliation du mérite avec de la fortune* (1665)—*Reconciliation of Merit and Fortune.* Motivated by financial awards from Louis XIV, Saint-Réal paid homage to his benefactor in the dialogue between Merit and Fortune, suggesting that the Sun King alone can reconcile intellectual excellence with worldly affluence. His need to court Louis XIV by incorporating propaganda favorable to French politics in his works would be intensified by the fact that the financial awards would cease after 1670 due to the war-related monetary reductions that would affect many men of letters. The *Réconciliation* also reveals the incipient moral pessimism that would infuse Saint-Réal's later works, and that, along with his exploration of history as an arena of moral examination, would begin to emerge more fully in his next work, the essay *De l'usage de l'histoire—Of the usage of history*. His experience as a foreigner in Paris pressured by the need for financial survival and eager to fit into society and into the intellectual circles where he felt he belonged, instilled in him the understanding of how basic personal motivations determine political actions, even if those actions contradict moral principles. Forced to suppress partisan opinions about his native land that might have been in conflict with Louis XIV's policies or critical of France's complicated relationship with the Duchy of Savoy, Saint-Réal committed himself to promoting the French political agenda. Before embarking on this propaganda in his first *nouvelle historique*, he articulated his views on the role of history in discerning human motivations, thus launching his exploration of the affinity between history and psychology in *De l'usage de l'histoire*.

In Saint-Réal's view, history is a mirror. It is the historical novel's duty to polish that mirror and endow it with magnifying qualities for readers to recognize their own flawed or virtuous motivations in the minutest detail. History is conducive to discernment between *la mauvaise gloire*—the acclaim garnered by the ostentatious display of knowledge without a real understanding of it—and *la véritable morale*, the true moral that comes from reflection and examination. The study of history should encourage independent judgment, and yet, Saint-Réal protests, in the education system it is merely a means to memorize dates and facts without allowing time for thought. This avidity for facts leaves no room for reflection. In complaining about education, Saint-Réal blames not only teachers but also parents whose goal is to have their children recite historical particulars and sound knowledgeable in order to impress their elders. The greatest defect of those who learn history only to fill up their memory and display knowledge is that, while they note the actions of historical personages, they are incapable of drawing their own conclusions about the reasons behind those very actions. The study of history should be used as a source of enlightenment because it offers a diverse context in which one can get to know human motivations, which remain, essentially, timeless. Once these motivations are understood in the past, they can be understood in the present. History teaches, as Saint-Rèal writes, that "one can meditate on men's actions usefully, and draw wise instructions even from the most unreasonable motivations that make them act... that there is nothing more equivocal than our actions, and that one must always go back to motives if one wants to know men: because it is in their motives that one properly gets to know their mind and the extent of what it is capable." Saint-Réal acknowledges the power of words to persuade and to deceive by giving a pleasant disguise to ugly facts. As signifiers, words can overpower reason and obscure the real meaning at their core, especially when one is reluctant to examine them. He offers the example of the word *Ligue* (League)—denoting la *Ligue Catholique* (the Catholic League)—a term that carries violent connotations for the Ottoman Empire. Behind its holy aura, this word signified war and hostilities to such an extent that the Turks did not hesitate to assist France's Henry IV in fighting the *Ligue* at the mere mention of it.

De l'usage de l'histoire gave Saint-Réal the opportunity to articulate what, aside from political propaganda, would be an important credo in writing *Dom Carlos, nouvelle historique*: history allows us to "penetrate the secret of hearts" and uncover "the spiritual anatomy of human actions." On this quest, Saint-Réal would reconstruct detailed thought processes behind the actions of the main characters in *Dom Carlos*. While striving to be a mimesis of historical texts, the *nouvelle*'s narrative reflects his continued preoccupation with the association between history and psychology.

In *Dom Carlos*, Saint-Réal's protagonists, Elisabeth de Valois, Dom Carlos, and King Philip II of Spain, are foremost historical personages portrayed with the human passions and inner conflicts that characterize the literary and dramatic works of the time, such as Madame de La Fayette's and Madame de Villedieu's novels, and Racine's plays *Bajazet* and *Bérénice*. Where Saint-Réal begins to challenge the *nouvelle historique* form is through his narrative. It is stripped of literary embellishments and unnecessary dialogue, imitating historical chronicles. He also provides a detailed list of sources that follows his *Avis*—brief foreword—as well as "Notes" within the text. This makes for a startling paradox: while Saint-Réal unsettles history in favor of the story, he simultaneously anchors his plot in history, thus operating within both fiction and fact. He stands out from other writers of his time because, in this narrative negotiation, he grants history a more official role than his contemporaries, especially through the filter of politics. The pivotal point of transformation that helps him break free from the standard blend of love and morality tales seasoned with historical particulars is *la conjuration*—the conspiracy—specifically, its political elements. While conspiracies are present in *Dom Carlos*—the Béarn conspiracy and the internal plot against Dom Carlos, the Infante—Saint-Réal's art of depicting a *conjuration* would develop fully in his next historical work, *Conjuration des espagnols contre la république de Venise—The Conspiracy of the Spaniards against the Republic of Venice*. In both *Dom Carlos* and *Conjuration des espagnols*, he creates a narrative world in which the political elements compete for attention with the story lines. The two works present Spain as a tyrannical, aggressive force whose leaders are willing to employ cruel and deceptive means to remain in power.

In the second half of the seventeenth century, a literary and historical interest in Spain developed among French literati. Historians like Brantôme, whose *Memoirs* appeared in 1665, gave accounts of Philip II, Don Carlos, Elisabeth, and Charles V, while translations of Spanish works, including those of Spain's Baroque theatre, made authors like Enciso, Lope de Vega, Montalbán, and their Spanish subjects familiar to French readers. By the 1670s, Spanish-Moorish themes were stimulating the imagination of French writers as seen in Madame de La Fayette's *Zayde* (1671) and Madame de Villedieu's *Galanteries grenadines* (1672-1673), works that rely on novelist Ginés Pérez de Hita's tales of life at court and the Granada wars. Among the many imaginative endeavors born of Iberian fascination, Saint-Réal's writing is unique in creating a more disabused image of Spain, not just historically but also in his descriptions of locations such as the Escorial, the San Yuste Monastery, and Guadalupe in Extremadura. His striving towards geographical and historical truthfulness reflected an ongoing competition with Madame de Villedieu and Madame de La Fayette. All three drew from Spanish literature and history to create a hybrid of *nouvelle galante* and *historique*, but it is Saint-Réal who tips the scale towards history while his two contemporaries favor amorous intrigues.

Novelist, historian, diplomat, and archivist, Saint-Réal was constantly enmeshed in a narrative negotiation between the historical and the novelistic. While history does play a more important role in his novel than in other *nouvelles historiques*, he nevertheless sacrifices certain facts in favor of romantic effects and dramatic conflicts. But he does so in a spirit of *vraisemblance*—verisimilitude—that is compactly intertwined with politics. The thwarted love story in *Dom Carlos*, one of the core elements in the enmity between father and son, is a pretext for the political clash that instigates the internal conspiracy against the Infante. Ruy Gomez, the Duke of Alba, Eboli, and the Inquisition are connected by their mutual goal to destroy the Spanish prince. Dom Carlos is as much a victim of this conspiracy as he is of his unhappy love. The negotiation between Saint-Réal the novelist and Saint-Réal the historian becomes a taut intermingling of verified historical facts and plausibility that makes it impossible for his contemporaries to distinguish history from fiction. The Savoyard writer tilts the angle of his vision by choosing historical sources with particular leanings, such as Protestant historians Turquet de

Mayerne, d'Aubigné, and de Thou. He omits certain details, mainly those depicted by Philip's official historiographer, Cabrera de Córdoba, to support his portrayal of Dom Carlos as a victim of his father, trapped into an impossible love.

Saint-Réal's narrative negotiation extends even further: between the fictional necessity for idealized heroes and psychological exploration. In the portrayals of Elisabeth and Dom Carlos, he creates a fusion of noble traits and flaws. The exposure of flaws is more acute in Elisabeth's case, but this is only to highlight, by contrast, how moral and wise she becomes in the course of the novel. What better propaganda for France than a portrayal of moral evolution and superiority amidst primitive Spanish passion and cruelty? The *Avis* presents the narration of this story as a defense of Elisabeth's virtuous and brave reputation, particularly in her involvement in foiling the Béarn conspiracy to kidnap the Protestant Queen of Navarre and her son, the future King of France, Henry IV. In the beginning, Saint-Réal depicts the French-born Spanish Queen as a flirtatious adolescent whose pleasure lies in being loved, and whose love is not as profound as that of Dom Carlos. For her, the effects of the broken engagement are not devastating. Until the change of fiancés, her main concern centers on the impact that her portrait may have on Dom Carlos and the hope that his emotional state is less calm than hers. After Elisabeth is engaged to Philip, her curiosity changes to worry that Dom Carlos may actually love her. Married by proxy by the Duke of Alba, she delays her arrival in Spain to allow time for reason and reality to calm both her fear and the infatuation of her new husband's son. On the other hand, Dom Carlos's belief that Elisabeth is experiencing the same ravaging emotions generate in him the delusion that will end up isolating him emotionally and mentally from other courtiers as well as from his own ambitions. It also gives the sense that Dom Carlos has constructed another reality in his mind, an impression that will deepen in the later treatments by Schiller and Verdi. Projection engenders isolation, and Saint-Réal's Infante remains trapped in this self-fashioned prison only to escape it in death. Nevertheless, he is portrayed as a classical hero. His mysterious end is depicted by Saint-Réal as a collaboration with his killers: he agrees to slice his veins in the bathtub.

The Infante is an embodiment of Stoic virtue, something that Elisabeth also possesses, even more markedly in her later portrayals by Schiller and Verdi. The Stoic cult of acceptance and the two protagonists' disenchantment with the world of the court reflect not only Saint-Réal's pessimism, but also his support of Louis XIV's hostility towards Spain. *Dom Carlos* was written, after all, between two wars led by the Sun King to claim territory in the Spanish Netherlands. The first war proved less than satisfactory for Louis XIV as he had to return most of the territories he had conquered. Elisabeth's transformation from superficial teenager into a model of virtue that confronts Philip's tyranny is a victory over the evil, abusive intolerance of the Spanish. As noted in Chapter One, Philip was a symbol of Spain itself in the "Black Legend" constructed around the Spanish empire, and served as the target of widespread Protestant, anti-Spain propaganda. By elevating Elisabeth to the level of symbol, Saint-Réal reflects the desired victory of France over Spain in the French-born Queen's moral triumph over the Spanish King. The publication of *Dom Carlos* could not have been better timed: its political agenda supports Louis XIV's disillusionment with the Spanish Netherlands campaign and his increased enmity towards Spain. Yet, as political as he intended to be,

Saint-Réal never dilutes his focus on the development and consequences of personal motivations. His detailed scrutiny of the emotions and thought processes that lead to actions makes *Dom Carlos* a true precursor of the psychological novel.

As the first *roman* to earn that designation, Madame de La Fayette's *La Princesse de Clèves* draws on the examination of passions through rational means to portray the interiority of the main character. The plot actually connects to Saint-Réal's *Dom Carlos* by depicting Elisabeth's by-proxy wedding to the Duke of Alba, and the selection of the Princesse of Clèves and her husband to accompany the new Spanish Queen on her journey towards Spain. In its brevity and substance, *La Princesse de Clèves* was an immediate success and became the focus of several debates over the heroine's confession to her husband. Critics accused the protagonist's behavior of being *invraisemblable*—improbable. Still, the novel exemplifies the century's preoccupation with succumbing to passion versus maintaining emotional and mental freedom. Through the protagonist's inner musings, readers encounter a heroine who possesses an in-depth grasp on the psychological, societal, political, and gender-related dynamics affecting a woman of her position. Her two fundamental choices—the confession and the ultimate rejection of the Duc de Nemours—are singular and surprising, given the behavior and elaborate maneuvers that occupied most other female characters of her milieu who often surrendered to *galanteries*. The court is presented as a minefield with historical accuracy in its description of events and intrigues—unveiled in detailed steps and analyses of thoughts similar to Saint-Réal's—in which an amalgam of desire and politics influences aristocratic life. The idea that a woman perceived the consequences of living such a life and refused to participate fully, despite her personal inclinations, was defiant and seemingly improbable. But it also demonstrated that a woman of the time could possess great self-mastery and the rational capability to distance her judgment from her emotions. This detachment enables the Stoic acceptance of unhappiness and disengagement from the world that is similarly represented in *Dom Carlos*. The Princesse de Clèves fortifies herself in her choice by adopting the path of isolation. Saint-Réal's Elisabeth also hints at the need for retreat, which will be further expressed in Schiller's and Verdi's portrayals. The Savoyard writer is rarely, if ever, credited with what has long been considered an original achievement of Madame de La Fayette's more famous novel which was, lest anyone forget, published six years after *Dom Carlos*: the elaborate interplay between sheer emotion and psychological insight.

As it does for the Princesse de Clèves, self-mastery proves a source of strength for Elisabeth. She displays cool shrewdness in influencing emotions. She convinces Dom Carlos to flee to Flanders by promising him that they would be able to meet unobserved when he returns, as his absence would have already alleviated existing suspicions about them. In fact, she wants to distance the Infante from her to prevent any damage caused by his barely-controllable passion. The disparate intensity of sentiments between Elisabeth and Dom Carlos, and the latter's delusion that she feels as he does but is making a great effort to dissimulate her love precipitate the Infante's downfall. They place him in a state of paralysis and inability to act. It is not surprising that Dom Carlos—especially in Schiller's version—has been referred to as another Hamlet. But while Hamlet's insanity is feigned and used as a defense mechanism, in Dom Carlos the delusion of love activates the already-existing seeds of mental instability, although Saint-Réal never refers to the documented madness of the Infante. The isolation through love begins for Dom Carlos through an infatuation with Elisabeth's portrait. He is betrothed to her when they are both not even teenagers during the truce established by his grandfather, Emperor Charles V, and her father, the French King Henri II. For three years, the Infante's imagination stirs his passion until the Treaty of Cateau-Cambrésis steals Elisabeth from him and offers her to the newly-widowed Philip. Saint-Réal describes the dashing of Dom Carlos's hopes as a devastating lightning bolt that enflames both his love and the already-existing inner rage against his emotionless father, aggravated by his inability to control his fate. In Hamlet-fashion, this powerlessness eventually turns the Infante's despair into melancholy and a perpetual state of indecision. His delusional love for Elisabeth intensifies a sense of alienation whose roots run deep into a childhood without a mother and without the affection of a father. In fact, the father-son relationship borders on sado-masochism: the only way the Infante can get his father's attention is to do something to provoke being punished. This dynamic will be similar in Schiller's play, which will also highlight the Infante's awareness of Philip's murderous power: at age six, he witnesses his father sign four death warrants. In making it clear that Dom Carlos has always suffered from the severity and austerity of his father, Saint-Réal omits any historical mention of paternal concern. Philip is depicted as an inhuman tyrant who swallows all of his son's amorous hopes: as Chronos, he devours his son, not only by depriving him of his fiancée and his political, military ambitions, but also of his life. Saint-Réal's King constantly misunderstands his son. As much as the Infante tries to disguise his chagrin at having lost Elisabeth, his frustrated demeanor is interpreted by Philip as an impatient desire to dethrone him and seize the crown. Dom Carlos has never felt loved by his father. The Infante remains a perpetual infant in constant hunger for a never-known mother and an inaccessible father. Elisabeth becomes the substitute for—and target of—all the missing love in his life. The ease with which one can slip into a psychological reading of Saint-Réal's novel attests to the affinity between history and psychology exploited by the author. The stretching of facts allows for the dilation of the private sphere, which enables Saint-Réal to create the simultaneously intimate and grand portrayals of his characters within the tension of the interplay between historical accuracy and fiction.

Dramatic conflict thrives on such tension. In reality, Elisabeth sees Dom Carlos only after she meets Philip. In the novel, Dom Carlos greets her on her journey to Madrid where she will see the King for the first time. This causes her much agitation but also gives Saint-Réal the opportunity to describe the Infante through her eyes. Schiller will not show any form of an initial meeting but will indicate that Don Karlos has fallen in love with Elisabeth after returning from his studies eight months before the play's beginning. Verdi's five-act version of the opera will set this encounter in the Fontainebleau woods where Elisabeth will discover that the Spanish stranger assisting her while her page has gone to find her attendants, is not an ambassador but the Infante himself. The portrait he gives her will later act as the trigger of Philip's jealous rage. Borrowing from Brantôme's account, Saint-Réal hints at the historical truth of the Infante's deformities—"Dom Carlos wasn't regularly well-built"—yet adds that he had the most beautiful head in the world with fiery, intelligent eyes. With a polite, ambiguous remark, the Savoyard writer creates a pact between his fictional need for a noble hero and historical truth: "one could not say that he was unpleasant." During the carriage ride to Madrid, Elisabeth and Dom Carlos contemplate one other in silence. A more faithful, albeit imaginative, interpreter than history as Saint-Réal would have it, the gaze is significant in Elisabeth's first encounter with Philip as well. Lost in her thoughts, she stares at the King for too long, and he, nervously, asks her whether it is his white hair that she is noticing. The age difference becomes Philip's obsession and one of the main factors that undermine his relationship with the young Queen. It plays a role in Elisabeth's disappointment that Philip is not behaving as tenderly and demonstratively towards her as a newlywed in love. Her beauty and grace, in such contrast to Spanish austerity, are immediately adored by the court and by Philip himself, although he never relinquishes his severity, and withholds affection in public. Saint-Réal masterfully describes the consequences of Philip's repression: by restricting all his tenderness and love to the confines of the bedroom at night, the King's love becomes violently passionate and possessive, trapping him into his own mental prison of suppression and doubt. But his coldness during the day makes him, in Elisabeth's eyes, seem enamored only of his own political stratagems. An immediate emotional misunderstanding installs itself between Elisabeth and Philip, and this sets the tone for their alienation from each other, which fuels the dramatic conflict. She interprets his reserve as indifference and, to appease her youthful need for affection and tenderness, finds a measure of fulfilment in the Infante's ardor. But, true to the French ideal of mastery of passions, Elisabeth's pleasure at being flattered soon subsides, turning to pity for Dom Carlos's torments; she asks him to avoid her. While Saint-Réal, a skilled explorer of human nature, has his qualms about his century's extolling of reason—he explains that even reason and virtue can be disguises for love to insinuate itself within a heart—he never shows Elisabeth as losing her head. In her conversations with the Infante at court, she speaks of her childhood while he elaborates on his passion for her. Elisabeth refrains from discussing their broken betrothal or anything that might trigger the Infante's ardor, and Dom Carlos, in full projection mode, reads a painful suppression of feelings in her reserved manner.

Saint-Réal's insistence on portraying Dom Carlos as a knightly hero victimized by the Inquisition leads him to idealize not only his physical appearance but also several biographical aspects that tamper with history, such as the Infante's close relationship with his grandfather, Charles V. In retreat from the world, Charles V has softened his intolerance towards the Protestant religion. The former emperor is surrounded by three spiritual advisors, Augustín Cazalla, Bartolomé de Carrenza y Miranda, archbishop of Toledo, and Constantin Ponce, the bishop of Drosse and Charles' confessor. After Charles' death, they are accused of heresy for having influenced the emperor to write, according to the Inquisition, an anti-Catholic will. Inspired by Philip's zeal to defend Catholicism—considered the true religion—from Protestant beliefs referred to as "new opinions," the Inquisitors attack and destroy those who have last seen the emperor alive and heard his confession. As the rest of Europe condemns the convictions of the three spiritual advisors, Philip stops the Inquisitors from burning the emperor's will, which would have further increased the outrage. Here Saint-Réal weaves in the legend about the bond between Charles V and Dom Carlos. He envisions a friendship between the two, presenting the grandfather as a major influence on the

Infante's dreams of glory and future interest in Flanders. The bond between the former emperor and Dom Carlos will be given a mythical quality in Verdi's opera: Charles V's spirit disguised as a monk will save the Infante from Philip and the Inquisition by taking him into the San Yuste Monastery. Although Verdi will dislike settling for this supernatural ending, through it he will, consciously or not, establish a direct connection to Saint-Réal's fictionalized relationship between Charles V and his grandson. The attachment to his grandfather spurs Dom Carlos to protest publicly the sentence of burning the emperor's testament. He allies himself with Dom Juan of Austria—the bastard son of Charles V, and Philip's half-brother—and with the Prince of Parma in this act of defiance against the Inquisition and threatens to destroy the Holy Office, which places him irrevocably on the Inquisitors' black list. To alleviate the tensions increased by the resentment of the population towards the church-defying Infante, further incensed by the Inquisitors' effective spreading of rumors, Philip sends his son to the famed university in Alcalá to keep him out of sight for a time. Here Saint-Réal introduces the character based on the real-life hero, Count Egmont.

Born into the Flemish aristocracy, honored by Charles V, and named general steward of Flanders, Egmont refuses to fight the Huguenots and the Flemish who are protesting the introduction of the Inquisition. This act of defiance would bring him to a tragic end despite the glories he achieved for Spain at the battles of Saint-Quentin and Gravelines. In Saint-Réal's novel it is Egmont who embodies the role that the Marquis of Posa will play in the adaptations by Schiller and Verdi: the catalyst behind the Infante's decision to embrace the Flemish cause. Dom Carlos befriends Egmont during the trip to Alcalá. Fascinated by the latter's battle stories, he decides to learn the art of war from him. The Alcalá sojourn provides the opportunity for another variation on history: the fictionalizing of Dom Carlos's fall that caused the famous head injury and near-death illness whose development was watched with interest by all European courts. Saint-Réal chooses to keep his hero knightly and has him tumble from a horse rather than draw on the historically-documented account of his fall down the stairs while chasing a young girl to fulfill his sadistic inclinations. The real version would hardly suit the victim of unfulfilled love that Saint-Réal intends to offer his readers. There is also no mention either of the trepanation procedure performed by renowned doctor and anatomist Andreas Vesalius or of the Infante's miraculous revival attributed to the remains of Franciscan friar Diego de Alcalá brought to him on the day before his recovery. In reality, the people of Spain prayed for Dom Carlos's life. In the novel, they consider this accident a just punishment from God for protesting the Inquisition's decision to burn Charles V's testament, and it is Elisabeth's letter that saves the Infante by instilling in him the will to live. In this context Saint-Réal introduces the Marquis of Posa who acts not only as the carrier of correspondence between Dom Carlos and Elisabeth, but also as their confidant, which precipitates his unfortunate end. Posa and Dom Carlos establish a rare friendship between a prince and a courtier, based on mutual admiration. The former's discretion and mastery of self—he does not lose his head over Elisabeth as do most others—enable him to be a constant presence around the Queen to the envy of court members who begin to suspect them of an affair. Meanwhile, the Queen's pregnancy becomes the tool for Alba and Ruy Gomez to push Philip's jealousy over the edge. The King suspects Posa of being the father of Elisabeth's unborn baby, and enraged by further open gallantries between the Marquis and Queen, he orders the assassination of Posa.

Despite his assistance, Saint-Réal's Posa remains a minor character. It is Schiller who, also drawing on the character of Egmont, will transform the Marquis into the embodiment of a principle—freedom of thought—and the advocate of the Flemish cause. Verdi will follow Schiller in his representation of Posa's idealism and self-sacrifice to save Don Carlos. Both playwright and composer will create one of the most dramatically-effective, politically-charged dialogues/duets of their œuvres: the confrontation between Posa and Philip. The diplomatic Saint-Réal might have played it safe in choosing Egmont as the instigator of Dom Carlos's defiance of his father. Egmont existed in history, therefore his portrayal as a subversive would not jeopardize Saint-Réal's position as it could not be attributed to his own imagination and political beliefs. Not to mention that Spanish oppression and cruelty stood out even more in contrast to Egmont's bravery and services to Spain when the Duke of Alba executed him. Thus, in Saint-Réal's diplomatically—and financially—motivated work, Egmont is both rebel and instrument in denigrating Spain whereas Schiller and, to a lesser extent, Verdi will use the Egmont-inspired Posa to transmit political messages motivated by their own ideals. The artist's condition will orient talent in any direction, be it protest or the securing of existence. What for Saint-Réal is a tool of diplomacy will become a tool of artistic evolution for Schiller and Verdi.

When Dom Carlos returns to Madrid from Alcalá, Saint-Réal gives us hints of madness in his behavior. The pregnant Elisabeth observes the Infante's unreasonable jealousy: "he was making such bizarre and unreasonable complaints that anyone else but her would have thought that he had lost his mind." These indications of irrationality and emotional instability combined with his gullible nature and enviable position as inheritor of Philip's crown make the Infante an easy target for conspiracy. Saint-Réal develops the conspiracy theme in *Dom Carlos* by constructing external and internal machinations that interconnect and nourish each other. After Elisabeth foils the plot to kidnap the Protestant Queen of Navarre, Jeanne d'Albret, and her son, the future Henry IV, she becomes a suspect along with Dom Carlos who had not been involved in the plan. This external conspiracy serves to deepen the net of intrigues that constitute the internal conspiracy leading to the downfall of both Queen and Infante. Here is where Saint-Réal excels at anchoring his plot into history: by embedding the emotional and psychological dramatic elements within the political interplay of the forces at work in a conspiracy, he makes it difficult to separate fiction from historical fact and to contest and/or dismiss either. His source for the Béarn plot is historian Jacques Auguste de Thou's *Historia sui temporis*.

The Duke of Alba, one of the main designers of the conspiracy, assigned a certain captain Dominique to kidnap the Queen of Navarre and her son, who were residing in Pau in Béarn, and bring them before the Spanish Inquisition. Historically, Jeanne d'Albret had already been warned by her cousin, Cardinal Georges d'Armagnac, the Papal legate who had baptized her son, the future Henry IV, and who was a protector of Catholicism among the Huguenots. In his letter, the Cardinal implored the Queen of Navarre to restore what had been pillaged from the churches at Lescar and Pau on her orders, alerting her to the dangers of her behavior: "You are being misled by evil counsellors who seek to plant a new religion in Béarn and Basse Navarre. You will never succeed because your subjects will not stand for it... Your neighbors will intervene. Spain will not tolerate a different religion between her borders, nor France within... Join the great lords, momentarily seduced, but now striving to exterminate these seditious heretics. Join them and save Navarre for your son." In a bold reply, Jeanne countered the Cardinal's reproaches accusing him of being blinded by "the honors of Rome." She refused to recognize the authority of the Pope's legate in Béarn, and claimed that she was not "planting a new religion but restoring an old one." The Cardinal's warning came to fruition in Philip's conspiracy whose historically-documented construction was elaborately deceptive.

As Captain Dominique arrived in Spain to receive orders from the Duke of Alba, he fell ill and was cared for by one of Elisabeth's servants, Vespier, to whom he confessed the plan. Vespier relayed the captain's confession to Elisabeth's grand almoner, the abbé St. Etienne, who warned his Queen. Elisabeth immediately wrote a coded letter to the French ambassador, Everard de Saint-Sulpice, revealing the plot. Saint-Réal attributes this interference to the glory that the Fates had in store for Henry IV: "...the great destinies of the young prince pre-empted such a well-organized attempt. They kept him to become, one day, the guardian of France and the terror of the Spanish." He praises Elisabeth as a determinant of those Fates: "...without her, the Prince of Navarre would have never become the greatest king in the world..." In foiling this conspiracy, the French-born Queen followed the inclination of her heart and Saint-Réal proved his point: Elisabeth's personal motivations determined the course of history.

With the Béarn conspiracy, Saint-Réal practiced his hand for his later *Conjuration des espagnols contre la République de Venise*. This account begins with an evocation of one of the Béarn conspiracy targets, Henry IV. As King of France, he resolved the conflict between Pope Paul V and the Republic of Venice, convincing the Holy See to lift the Venetian Interdict—a successful outcome for the Venetians that aroused the anger of Spain. Henry's death opens the way for Spain to express hostility, and the Spanish ambassador's—the Marquis of Bedmar—conspiracy plan emerges as a vehicle of internal attack directed at the leadership of the Republic: the Venetian Council of Ten and the Senate. Saint-Réal's narrative steers clear of amorous intrigues and focuses solely on the conspiracy. The woman character, a Greek courtesan, plays a key role: she lodges some of the conspirators in her quarters and facilitates their activities. Machiavelli's influence on Saint-Réal is evident: his warning in *The Prince* that a sovereign must be circumspect when hiring soldiers who have no native loyalty proves true. Venice's mercenary troops resent the Republic for being treated badly, and are easy to manipulate into joining the army of the conspirators whose reasoning is presented as noble by one of the leaders, Renault. In a motivating speech, Renault declares that this conspiracy is meant to save the oppressed and restore peace, innocence, and liberty—"*la paix, l'innocence, et la liberté*"—in the corrupt Republic. Ultimately, another of the leaders, Jaffier, reveals the plot to the Venetian Doge and the Council of Ten, because he is touched by compassion when he witnesses the customary ceremony of the new Doge's marriage to the sea and experiences the serene joyfulness of the unsuspecting population, as Saint-Réal concludes "…heaven did not want to abandon the work of twelve centuries and so many wise minds to the fury of a courtesan and a troop of lost men."

Saint-Réal strives to keep his second *nouvelle historique* devoid of emotion and focused solely on history. Nevertheless, it is a human being's internal conflict—between pity for Venice and concern for his companions— that acts as the historical turning point leading to the foiling of the conspiracy and the destruction of most of its leaders. In an ironic twist, Bedmar escapes unharmed by virtue of his position, and declares that Spain fights only in the open and would never need to resort to underhanded methods. Meanwhile, the savior of Venice, Jaffier, in an emotional reversal after seeing that the Council did not respect the arrangement to spare his companions, joins a remaining faction, is captured, and executed. Saint-Réal remains true to his mission: to penetrate the secret of hearts and to demonstrate again that history is determined by very personal motivations. Conspiracies are even more revealing in this respect, he writes: they constitute "history's most moral and instructive sites." He considers them the greatest of men's enterprises because they demand of its participants courage, precaution, and loyalty, qualities that are often not all encountered in one person. As each conspiracy is so specific to its time, place, planners, and participants, one is responsible, when narrating them, for a rigorous attention to historical fact and detail. Confined to the internal psychology of the plot's actors, creative liberty and fiction can thus find their place within these firm lines of specificity without detracting from historical accuracy. This is where Saint-Réal unequivocally affirms the "historical" in the historical novel. He demonstrates that, while he may not be taken seriously as a historian, he is, by all means, not only a novelist. Through his representation of conspiracies he carves his own way into both history and literature. He creates a unique niche for his work that will largely be overlooked, even though his innovative hybrid will influence a great number of authors.

Saint-Réal is not the first seventeenth-century writer interested in conspiracies. In 1651, the poet Jean François Sarrazin, also known as Sarasin, wrote *La Conjuration de Valstein*, a prose narrative that appeared posthumously in 1656. In 1657 an anonymous work entitled *La conjuration du comte de Fiesque* was published in Paris and later claimed by Jean François Paul de Gondi, cardinal de Retz, in his *Mémoires*, as a text he had written in 1632. Another account, initially attributed to Saint-Réal, *Histoire de la conjuration des Gracques*, that appears in a five-volume collection of his *Œuvres posthumes* in 1722, is actually of uncertain authorship since many texts included in the collection were in fact written by Saint-Évremond, Le Noble or La Rochefoucauld. The prototype for these works is *The Conspiracy of Catiline* by Sallust, one of the earliest-known Roman historians whose works have survived. Sallust was the first to infuse the writing of history with dramatic narrative, moral reflection, and a certain partisanship on the part of the author. Despite his political agenda, Saint-Réal does not transmit only hostility towards Spain in his *Conjuration*: his description of Bedmar is filled with admiration. The Savoyard writer aspired towards political mastery, as did the cardinal de Retz. With *La conjuration du comte Jean-Louis de Fiesque*, Retz inspired Saint-Réal: in his account of Gianluigi Fiesco's conspiracy against Andrea Doria, the Republic of Genoa, trapped between the interests of Milan, France, and Spain, resembles the Venice of Saint-Réal's *nouvelle*. Retz was also a source for Schiller who, before claiming the Don Carlos story adaptation spotlight, will strive to establish his reputation as a playwright with his second play, *Fiesco's Conspiracy at Genoa (Die*

Verschwörung des Fiesco zu Genua), that will premiere four years before *Don Karlos, Infant von Spanien.* The seventeenth-century fascination with conspiracies was connected with personal aspirations. Both the Machiavelli-influenced, politically-involved Retz and Saint-Réal must have had an ideal of the perfect politician and admired those who excelled at politics regardless of what side they supported. But they could also imagine the possible repercussions were they to address the conspiracies of their time. By choosing foreign or historically-remote subjects, and sometimes publishing anonymously, they maintained a safe distance from potential incriminations during the absolute reign of the Sun King. Historical works were encouraged to serve as veiled propaganda in support of the King and France.

Eighteenth-century historians were keen to break up the union of history and literature, an endeavor that led to a "positivist philosophy" of history in the nineteenth century. However, narrated history cannot easily resist the association with fiction in order to present a complete, readable account, as long as the fiction lies within the borders of verisimilitude— *vraisemblable.* It is the *le vraisemblable* that bridges contradictory or disjointed historical facts. The conspiracy narrative then, in its historical specificity and succinctness of action, provides the ideal medium for writers to color within the lines of fact and fiction, and create a reciprocally-supportive relationship between history and verisimilitude. Saint-Réal's revelation of the secrets of personal motivations implies a revelation of historico-political secrets and vice versa. This uncovering of secrets is why conspiracy accounts appealed to readers of the time and proved very successful. Through the conspiracy narrative Saint-Réal develops what is, arguably, the most tightly-knit bond that history and literature can form.

From the international stage of conspiracies Saint-Réal moves to the microcosm of conspiracies at home to depict the nuanced weaving of the plot against Dom Carlos. It is the Infante's love for Elisabeth that places him in a position of great vulnerability. A primary layer of machinations is already in place. Aside from a political alliance with Dom Carlos in the protest against the burning of Charles V's testament, Dom Juan of Austria's closeness to the Infante is, not surprisingly, motivated by personal agendas. Smitten with Elisabeth, Dom Juan perceives the Infante's love for his stepmother, and is eager to discover more. He flatters the gullible prince to gain his confidence. Meanwhile, he embarks on an affair with the Princess of Eboli, the wife of Dom Carlos's former tutor, Ruy Gomez. Famous for her beauty and power of seduction, the princess, whose advances have been rejected by the Infante, welcomes the alliance to Dom Juan to satisfy her own desire for vengeance. She is jealous of Elisabeth and curious to discern the Queen's feelings for Dom Carlos.

Added to this layer of sexual jealousies is the political fear that Dom Carlos would gain power if sent to govern Flanders. The main strategist of the Béarn conspiracy, the Duke of Alba, shares this apprehension with Ruy Gomez. Aided by Eboli, the two contribute to distancing the Infante even more from his father. At first, they do not consciously plan to endanger Dom Carlos's life. But as the King becomes increasingly doubtful of Alba's abilities due to the failed Béarn conspiracy, the two partners in crime advance step by step towards a murderous revenge. Profiting from Elisabeth's pregnancy, they succeed in keeping her away from Philip as well. Assisted by another personage drawn from real life, the secretary of state, Antonio Pérez, they use every moment to defend Alba and denigrate the Queen and the Infante. As Alba cannot believe Elisabeth capable of being so clever as to foil a conspiracy, he is convinced that Dom Carlos helped her, and communicates these suspicions to the King. This alliance of three conspirators against Dom Carlos—Gomez, Alba, and Pérez—is a precursor of the *Conjuration des espagnols* trio: Marquis of Bedmar, Duke of Osuna, and Don Pedro de Toledo. Philip's jealousy becomes both sexual and political: he recalls the initial betrothal of the Queen to his son and suspects that they love each other, while also remembering her preference for France as superior in all matters. The arrival of the Flemish deputies, Marquis de Bergh and Baron of Montigny, precipitates the downfall of Dom Carlos and Elisabeth. Verdi will set the Flemish deputies' plea—addressed directly to the King—and the Infante's request to be sent to Flanders, within an *auto-da-fé* scene. The human plight of an oppressed people alongside the spectacle of cruelty that is the burning of heretics will amplify the sense of Philip's power and tyranny. While Schiller will not show the *auto-da-fé*, the public display of immolation will be a pretext for Philip's tyranny to manifest in private as well: Elisabeth will plead with him to spare her the horror of attending, but he will force her to go, questioning her faith.

For Saint-Réal's Dom Carlos, the meeting with the Flemish deputies is an awakening. At last he realizes that he has been paralyzed by his forbidden love and has accomplished nothing on the path to gaining glory. After this encounter, Dom Carlos, while inspired, is still not resolved to leave, and it is here where Elisabeth intervenes as the force of shrewd reason to persuade him to embrace his mission. Emboldened by her support, Dom Carlos declares himself publicly in favor of the Flemish nobility, scandalizing the Inquisitors who had not forgotten his previous defiance. Uncharacteristically diplomatic, Philip promises to take his son to Flanders himself out of concern for his safety, but he delays the departure by feigning illness. Yet he cannot dupe either Elisabeth or Dom Carlos. Saint-Réal introduces an ironic streak in the Infante—this sense of irony will come to full bloom in Schiller's portrayal—as he mocks Philip's world travels and creates a small booklet parodying the King's limited, mainly local voyages: from Madrid to the Escorial, from the Escorial to Toledo, from the Prado to the Escorial. Eboli succeeds in copying the booklet and gives the original to Ruy Gomez, while Elisabeth burns the counterfeit, mistaking it for the original. As Philip's feigned illness turns real, he misunderstands the Infante's intentions even more. When he notices him constantly present at his bedside, he believes that his son is exerting silent pressure on him to allow him to go to Flanders, when, in fact, Dom Carlos is there only to see Elisabeth who does not leave her sick husband's side.

Finally, the mocking travel booklet plays its role in solidifying Philip's suspicions about the close relationship between Dom Carlos and Elisabeth. Saint-Réal employs a veritable psychological novel approach, analyzing gestures, thoughts, inner transformations, and associations as Philip tries to guess who between Posa and the Infante was Elisabeth's confidant and who the lover. In the meantime, the united Flemish nobility instigates the plundering of churches, forcing the King to send the Duke of Alba there with troops. Dom Carlos, who believed he would have mastered the rebellions, plans to flee to Flanders in secret and stacks himself with weapons, but Dom Raymond of Taxis, the postmaster general, warns Philip that horses are being prepared for an escape at night.

In the meantime, Count Egmont and Count Horn have turned themselves in to the Duke of Alba relying on the redeeming virtues of their previous merits in service of Spain to be spared, but Alba has them executed. Saint-Réal fictionalizes history again as the real execution of Egmont and Horn occurred after the Infante's arrest. In the dramatic scene of Dom Carlos's incarceration, the Infante attempts suicide by throwing himself into the fire after the King with Ruy Gomez and others enter, but he is caught in time and condemned to live boarded up in his room with only a mattress for furniture and a mourning outfit as attire. To be surrounded by evocations of death and prevented from seeing any loved ones, friends or servants, is only the first stage of Philip's cruel punishment in Saint-Réal's ending.

Counting on the Inquisitors' grudges against the Infante, in all three treatments—novel, play, and opera—the King employs religion as an excuse for sacrificing his son and is laudably compared to Abraham and even God in his sacrifice. Schiller and Verdi will represent this religious approval of son-murder in the confrontation between Philip and the Grand Inquisitor, which, in its complex interplay of the blood-stained collaboration between church and monarchy, will become yet another of their most memorable scenes. In Saint-Réal's *Dom Carlos*, the discovery of incriminating papers alongside Elisabeth's letter to the prince while he was ill at Alcalá facilitates the Inquisition's investigation, and the Infante is accused of "new opinions." In Verdi's uncut version, there will be an impromptu trial of Don Carlos and Elisabeth with alternating accusations from Philip and the Grand Inquisitor, which will occur before the apparition of Charles V's ghost. Schiller's Philip will simply hand over his son to the Inquisition.

Saint-Réal creates a more elaborate finale. While Spain's population and European courts protest Dom Carlos's incarceration, the King, fearful of widespread public outrage, orders a slow-acting poison to be mixed in his son's food and smeared on his clothes. As the poison fails, the Infante is allowed to choose how to die. Saint-Réal defends his hero against historians who described him as weak, mentally unstable, and tantrum-prone by depicting his Stoic acceptance of death. The writer settles on one of the many versions reported by historians and ambassadors: the suicide by vein-cutting in a bath. This is a death befitting a hero, followed by a glorifying funeral. During the procession, his holy persecutor, Cardinal Spinoza, is publicly insulted. The fitting inscription on the Mausoleum portal attests to the Infante as a victim taken from life for fear that the evil of the century would seduce his mind, and describes him as "incomparable in greatness of soul, liberality, and love of truth." The heroic truth, as Saint-Réal would have it, emerges in death with this concluding inscription. Philip's revenge continues: he poisons the pregnant Elisabeth and appears at her bedside in mourning while she suffers pangs of death. Influenced by Princess Eboli who becomes his mistress, Philip has Dom Juan poisoned as well. But in Greek-tragedy fashion, Saint-Réal turns the Fates on all those responsible for the deaths of Dom Carlos and Elisabeth, except for the Duke of Alba who is last mentioned as he sentences Counts Egmont and Horn to death. After Princess Eboli's intrigues are unmasked, she is incarcerated for the rest of her life, while Philip dies suffocated by his ulcer.

Aside from Turquet de Mayerne, de Thou, d'Aubigné, Cabrera de Córdoba, Saint-Réal's historical sources included Matthieu, Brantôme, and Antonio Pérez. Most likely he had read the Spanish plays of the time, such as Enciso's *El Príncipe Don Carlos* in which the dramatic conflict centered on the tyrannical father aided by the zealous Inquisition versus an ill-fated son, and the Queen is not mentioned. Saint-Réal is the first to introduce the love story between Dom Carlos and Elisabeth. Infatuation nurtured by imagination enflamed by a portrait turns into love at first sight in Saint-Réal's *nouvelle* as it will in Schiller's play and Verdi's opera. The loss of this love's potential happiness will engender the sadness that Dom Carlos must sublimate into becoming the defender of Flemish freedom. Schiller and Verdi will make the Infante more obsessive, even aggressive, in his hope to regain Elisabeth. Dom Carlos's sublimation of passion followed by his decision to finally act occurs too late in all three treatments. But had it happened sooner, it would not have allowed for the intricate net of conspiracy to develop around the Infante. In this trio of the Don Carlos story interpretations, Saint-Réal sets the stage for the inextricability of history, psychology, politics, love, and conspiracy that is embraced by both Schiller and Verdi. While the German playwright and the Italian composer do not address foreign conspiracies, they do depict the internal plots against the politically-subversive Posa and the Infante. Love is the catalyst for this subversion and, as a consequence, for the conspiracies at home.

Saint-Réal's concept of the historical novel is unquestionably unique. As *Dom Carlos, nouvelle historique* traveled through time and adaptations, it may have lost acknowledgement and even recognition as an original source, but it always maintained its power to inspire. The premiere of Verdi's *Don Carlos* reawakened interest in the novel. A century later, history repeated itself, and the opera reaffirmed its capacity to bring this first novelistic treatment back into the spotlight: André Lebois' 1964 critical edition, entitled *Don Carlos, nouvelle historique*, was motivated by a major revival of Verdi's opera at the l'Opéra de Paris in March 1963. Again, Verdi's masterpiece closed the circle in the series of previous adaptations by restoring attention to the long-obscured chef-d'œuvre that is Saint-Réal's *Dom Carlos*. Since 1964, *Dom Carlos, nouvelle historique* has been published in nine editions.

CHAPTER 3

Friedrich Schiller: *Don Karlos, Infant von Spanien*
"Nenne mich Du"[*]

When Saint-Réal's *Dom Carlos, nouvelle historique* appeared in a German translation in 1784, Schiller had already read the novel in French and was working on his treatment of the Don Carlos story. It was a time of uncertainty for the German poet. In 1782, Schiller had left Stuttgart, where he worked as a regiment doctor, to escape the despotic rule of Duke Karl Eugen and pursue a career as a writer. During his studies at Karlsschule Stuttgart, the exclusive military academy founded by the Duke, Schiller had discovered the works of Rousseau and Goethe, and been inspired by the former's belief in Nature and the latter's explorations of subjectivity. He had also read the Classics and Shakespeare. All of these literary influences would contribute to the creation of his liberal and revolutionary model eventually embodied by the Marquis of Posa. While still a student, Schiller had written his first play, *Die Räuber* (1781)—*The Robbers*—whose critical perspective of social immorality and advancement of revolutionary ideals were remarkable for a novice playwright. *Die Räuber* was an instant success. But it incurred the Duke's persecution as the young playwright had left the regiment without

---

[*] Name me You (*Don Karlos*, 78).

permission to attend the play's premiere in Mannheim. The Duke sentenced Schiller to two weeks in prison, and decreed that he should present to him all of his written works for approval as they developed. Schiller's escape journey to protect his literary future took him through Frankfurt, Mannheim, Leipzig, and Dresden to Weimar, where he settled in 1787.

In the 1780s there were hardly any established venues for theatres in the German principalities. Plays were either performed in French at court or in the vernacular by traveling acting troupes. The first German national theatre was founded in Hamburg in 1767. A growing cultural nationalism animated a widespread desire to equal the reputation of French theatre. Theatre was an ideal forum for the German language to act as a unifying factor among the principalities. This cultural nationalism was guided by the Enlightenment ideal of fighting prejudice and oppression based on class differences. Gotthold Lessing's groundbreaking work on drama, *Hamburgische Dramaturgie* (1767), established the field of dramaturgy and presented theatre as a potential channel for the propagation of humanistic ideals. Through his plays and critical writings, Lessing contributed to the development of a new form of theatre, attacking the rigidity of French Neoclassical dramas and influencing the literary movement *Sturm und Drang*—*Storm and Stress*—in its rejection of rules and rationalism. In *The Sorrows of Young Werther* (1774), Goethe catalyzed the proliferation of the *Sturm und Drang* ideal of freedom in expressing subjectivity and emotional extremes. Two years later, the term *Sturm und Drang* appeared as the title of a play by Friedrich Klinger and became the official denomination of this early Romantic literary movement. With *Die Räuber*, Schiller made an important artistic contribution to the advancement of *Sturm und Drang* aesthetics and influenced the development of theatrical melodrama.

In his second play, *Die Verschwörung des Fiesco zu Genua* (1783)—*Fiesco's Conspiracy at Genoa*—Schiller focused on depicting the real Fiesco's 1547 conspiracy, while in his third, *Kabale und Liebe* (1784)—*Intrigue and Love*—he returned to *Sturm und Drang* models but gave a more complex dimension to romantic love. This return was not so much motivated by an artistic belief in *Sturm und Drang* concepts, but rather by Schiller's perceptions of his public as less interested in politics than in love stories. Schiller was ahead of his audiences and many of his contemporary writers in his preoccupation with how politics and government directly affect human happiness, and in his striving to explore larger, public concerns through his dramas. This advanced socio-political perspective emerged in Schiller's theatre from the very beginning: *Die Räuber* highlights issues of moral responsibility and freedom while conveying social criticism and attacking the church, *Fiesco* reflects democracy's struggle against tyranny, and *Kabale und Liebe* criticizes the cruelty, immorality, and narcissism of the aristocracy. However, like Saint-Réal, Schiller was compelled to compromise and connect the transmission of these larger issues to personal motivations. To maintain the audience's interest, he invoked the human hearts behind social conditions, politics, and historical actions, and appealed to *Sturm und Drang* concepts for the personalization of principles and clashing forces.

These concepts continued to inflect Schiller's writing as he began to adapt Saint-Réal's *Dom Carlos*. But there is a discernible shift that occurs after the first three acts. The remaining two acts are not as focused on Don Karlos and his unrestrained emotionality but rather on developing the characters of Posa as an agent of revolutionary idealism and of Philip as more complex than the one-dimensional tyrant of Saint-Réal's novel. This has been attributed to the fact that Schiller published the initial three acts in his literary journal, *Thalia*, after which he interrupted his writing to study historical sources. By this time Schiller was already pursuing the incipient transition from *Sturm und Drang* emotionality to the fusion of pre-Romanticism, Enlightenment, and Classicism that would form the *Weimarer Klassik—Weimar Classicism*—literary movement. During the break in writing, the playwright became more intent on transmitting political messages about the importance of free thought and the dangers of absolutism. He would be criticized later for inconsistencies between the first three acts and the following two as well as for the anachronism of the concepts represented by the Marquis of Posa's character. Schiller combatted such criticism in a series of twelve letters on *Don Karlos*, published in 1788 in *Der teutsche Merkur*. In the second letter, he addressed the comments that Posa's idealism would not have been conceivable during the reign of Philip II. The ideal of freedom is timeless and universal, and enlightened men like Posa could have existed even during the sixteenth century at the Spanish court: "…the most beautiful dreams of freedom are always dreamt in a dungeon… the most noble ideal of a human republic, general tolerance and freedom of conscience, where could these ideas have been born more easily and naturally than close to Phillip II and his Inquisition?... The time in which Posa is placed was just the time in which, more than ever before, human rights and freedom of conscience, were talked about. The preceding Reformation had first brought these ideas to the fore, and the unrest in Flanders kept them alive. His outer independence, his status as a Maltese Knight, provided him the opportunity to let his speculative yearnings ripen." *Don Karlos* created a platform for promoting an ideal humanity and encouraging evolution from the past. The German playwright thus moved from the criticism of class disparities and social abuses to the exposure of the evils of absolutism in both monarchy and institutionalized religion. In his letters, he wrote that *Don Karlos* is about "a favorite subject of our century, that of spreading purer, gentler humanity of feeling, that of the highest possible personal freedom in a flourishing, functioning state, in short, that of the most perfect condition of mankind, as it is attainable, considering mankind's nature and its strengths." Man's freedom, both inner and external, proved a ubiquitous theme for Schiller, sometimes to the extent that he created characters whose questionable actions are excused in the name of that freedom: these are "sublime criminals."

In the gradual evolution from *Sturm und Drang* to *Weimarer Klassik*, the use of irony acts as a necessary transformative distinction. While giving expression to emotional extremes in the character of the Infante, Schiller relies on irony to create a distancing effect. In his later work, *On Naïve and Sentimental Poetry* (1795-1796), Schiller would explain mockery as a method used by the sentimental poet to point out the differences between reality and ideals. There are evidences of this notion in *Don Karlos*: the sardonic highlighting of an unsatisfactory reality goes beyond the sarcastic insinuation used, for example, by the King's confessor, Domingo, to attack and expose, and emerges in various ironic remarks of Don Karlos, Elisabeth, and Philip. These ironies serve not so much to wound the interlocutor as to reveal the distance and irreconciliation between the speaker's ideal reality and the truth of the situation. And the ironic revelation is directed more to the speaker's own self—and the audience—rather than to the participants in the conversation. Schiller's Don Karlos is a more astute and quick-witted character than Saint-Réal's Infante. His capacity for subtle yet biting irony displays a better understanding of reality and of human nature. Although he is still gullible and can fall prey to deception, particularly to Princess Eboli's wiles, he is portrayed as more discerning, and like Hamlet—to whom Schiller himself compared him—he is clever, mocking, and acutely perceptive. The spirit of irony arises from the very beginning: a weapon that Don Karlos wields to pierce through Domingo's insinuations. As Domingo attempts to discover the source of the Infante's brooding gloom over the past months, which even the pleasant stay in Aranjuez did not dispel, Don Karlos protects himself from inadvertently revealing his true feelings and feigns bitter feelings towards Elisabeth for ousting him from his father's heart. The serpentine Domingo hints at the Queen's overwhelming concern for the Infante during a jousting tournament, a panic that visibly subsided as she learned that it was Philip who had been wounded and not Don Karlos. Here begins the development of that rarefied ironic spirit that infuses the entire work: asked by Domingo whether he is wrapped in thought, the Infante replies: "In wonder, sir, that the king's merry confessor should own so rare a skill in the romancer's art."

Don Karlos is aware that he is spied on by Philip's minions and mistrusts everyone with the exception of his only friend: the Marquis of Posa, the amalgam between Saint-Réal's Egmont and Posa. This friendship was not easily won as the Infante reminds Posa in their Act I Scene II encounter: when they were children he took the blame for a childish mistake that the Marquis committed—hurting the Infante's aunt during a game of badminton—and was whipped at his father's command. It took this sacrifice to convince Posa to drop his rules of protocol and allow himself to befriend the prince. Hints of Don Karlos's instability appear earlier and are more marked than in Saint-Réal's *nouvelle*, although delirious behavior and sudden oscillation between emotional extremes were not unusual for *Sturm und Drang* heroes. Upon his return from Brussels, Posa finds Don Karlos in a feverish state, and the Infante confesses his love for Elisabeth. After eight months of seeing her without being able to speak to her because of court protocol, he admits that this love is leading him to madness. Elements of the Infante's childhood are revealed in this first scene: Philip's contact with his son began when he was six years old, and, as in Saint-Réal's *nouvelle*, was limited only to moments of punishment. The King is depicted as frightening, cruel, and remote: Don Karlos recalls how he once saw his father sign four death warrants in one morning. The distortion of Nature is introduced here by the Infante. Don Karlos and his father are set against each other from the beginning as two opposite beings who share one yearning: "Nature could not in her wide orb have found two opposites more diverse in their elements. How could she bind the two extremes of human kind—myself and him—in one so holy bond?... Why should two men, in all things else apart, concur so fearfully in one desire?" Although father and son are bound by Nature, their bond is, paradoxically, unnatural as they are "two hostile stars that in the lapse of ages, only once, as they sweep onwards in their orbed course, touch with a crash that shakes them to the center" in their rival love for Elisabeth. The sense of resistance to biological ties is immediately established. And Nature is presented as a concept whose power to free humankind from the artifice of the status quo can also be turned on its own laws in the name of freedom. On one level, this reflects Rousseau's influence in advocating for Nature as the true source of wisdom. But on another level, it illustrates how, when a natural bond is transformed into a convention that serves as a pretext for tyranny, that natural bond must be set aside in order to undo the convention and escape the tyranny. For Schiller, the unlearning of convention appeals to Nature's freeing capacity yet goes beyond Nature in the name of total freedom.

Don Karlos expresses the desire to break his natural bond to his father, not by physical annihilation, but by the idea of unlearning the concept represented by that bond. He asks Posa a rhetorical question: "Should I forget the father—what were then the King to me?" The verb chosen by Schiller to signify "forget" is *verlernen* which literally means "to unlearn." This implies that the human concept of fatherhood is learned and neither inherent to blood ties nor naturally conducive to paternal or filial love. The word denotes the general struggle against learned concepts occurring not only within the dramatic art at the time, but also within the greater realm of literary movements. The aura of *verlernen* carries profound connotations. There is a general need for "unlearning" taking place in the movement away from *Sturm und Drang* ideals towards Weimar Classicism which facilitates a liberation from old precepts, although not a complete abandonment of them. This is not so much the unlearning of the precepts themselves as that of the boundaries between them. Weimar Classicism will come to represent a spirit of collaboration between movements that will bring together elements of early Romanticism, Classicism, and Enlightenment. It is a "scientific" Romantic union in defying convention: a defiance that is at once bold yet tempered by intellect, and respectful of classical principles.

The dilemma of Don Karlos represented in the struggle between abandonment to impulse and the rigidity of convention anticipates Schiller's *On the Aesthetic Education of Man in a Series of Letters*, published in 1794. These *Letters* contain a response to Immanuel Kant's *Critique of Judgment* (1790) by proposing a synthesis between the passive *Sinnestrieb* (the sensuous drive) and the active *Formtrieb* (the formal drive), the forces responsible for human beings' inner conflict between senses and reason. Schiller's concept of *Spieltrieb* (the play drive) as the solution that mediates the battle between the two opposing drives and results in "living form" is a conciliation of sensuous life and rationally-perceived or imposed forms. To achieve *Spieltrieb*, neither drive should be suppressed. On the contrary, the more freely one follows each drive and the greater the tension between them, the more profound and rewarding the experience of life, as Schiller writes: "Where both qualities are united, Man will combine the greatest fullness of existence with the utmost self-dependence and freedom, and instead of abandoning himself to the world, he will rather draw it into himself in the whole infinity of its phenomena and subject it to the unity of his reason." Form must move beyond the rational rigidity of abstraction and come to live in the emotions just as sensuous life must transcend the shapelessness of impulse to acquire form in man's understanding of the senses. The equilibrium between the two results in the highest ideal of beauty. Don Karlos's doom derives from his inability to explore and balance the two drives. He does not have the experience of achieving fulfillment by following either sheer impulse or elevated form: he is unable to live out his sexual desire for Elisabeth and he does not succeed in giving an aesthetically-satisfactory form to his life—such as embodying a man associated with glorious deeds: as the savior of Flanders, for instance. The Infante is perpetually trapped in between the two drives. His desire to unlearn his father is, in fact, a need to escape the fundamental elements that constitute the trap: the fatherhood and the monarchy of Philip.

This desire makes a complex and potent statement of the general spirit of defiance brewing in European consciousness in the late 1780s. If Don Karlos succeeds, he is not only unlearning the duties of a son but also those of a subject. It is a type of protest against that which is a given: being born to Philip implies it is a given that Don Karlos is his son. Living in the realm of King Philip II means it is a given that the Infante is both his father's political subject and his legal inheritor. What more powerful statement can Schiller make against that which is automatically embraced as the status quo? And why can't Nature itself be defied if its status quo is oppressive and destructive? Even natural laws can be unlearned. The use of "unlearn" here, whether Schiller consciously meant it so or not, is an homage to the power of reason to resist and deconstruct even the most fundamental, time-honored, naturally-bound concepts like the societally-conditioned expectations of behavior, as between father and son. And if that construct, rooted in such a close blood relation, can be undone by the power of the intellect, at least on an abstract level, then the dismantling of a cultural or political situation in favor of progress lies undisputedly within the capacity—and duty—of the enlightened mind. The concept of unlearning reflects an entire struggle versus the status quo.

As in Saint-Réal's *nouvelle*, Elisabeth is the voice of reason who tempers Don Karlos's passion and determines his decision to embrace the Flemish cause. From the moment she is introduced, she emerges as an intelligent woman guided by wisdom and compassion. Her remarks often seem to have a deeper meaning as though she is communicating her sorrow even to those she cannot trust. She understands Eboli's rejection of marriage to Ruy Gomez since the Princess does not love him —unlike in Saint-Réal's work, Eboli is not yet married—and one can instantly deduce Elisabeth's own plight as she declares: "'Tis a hard fortune to be sacrificed." There is also an immediate indication of the Queen's disdain for the inhuman austerity of Spanish court protocol. When she is reminded that she cannot see her daughter earlier than the scheduled hour, Elisabeth exclaims: "Not yet the hour for me to be a mother!" The distortion of Nature infiltrates every aspect of life at the Spanish court where strict rules force a mother to unlearn her instincts.

When Posa enters the scene from his recent trip to France and the Netherlands with letters from Elisabeth's mother, Schiller reveals that the Marquis and the Queen have known each other for some time: Posa had fought with Elisabeth's father, King Henry II at Rheims in a *Ritterspiel* (tournament) and won, wearing her colors, three times. In Schiller's first version of *Don Karlos* (1787) there is an exchange between Posa and Elisabeth that is cut in the second version (1802): Elisabeth comments on how easy it is to be a queen to which Posa replies: "Certainly, if one was born into it!" The Marquis expresses the given reality of royal blood genealogy: there is no question that royal blood ties imply the right to rule. Elisabeth responds that the world has corrupted Posa and that she cannot recognize in him the philosopher who would fearlessly speak the truth to the Throne. In her words, there is an implication of reproach that Posa is settling too easily for the status quo. Schiller's cuts for the 1802 version and the subsequent one of 1805 were influenced not only by the transition between literary movements, but also by practicality—to shorten the length of the play. Napoleon's rise may have also inspired some of the cuts. A member of the minor nobility becoming the first Emperor of France certainly represented an overturning of the legitimate royal blood requirement.

Posa surprises Elisabeth into actually meeting with the Infante who appears on the scene without the Queen having a chance to consider this encounter and strengthen her resolve. Despite her protests, Don Karlos remains in her presence to speak to her of his love and unhappiness. In this first meeting between Elisabeth and the Infante, the Queen defends Philip as father and husband. Don Karlos should not pity her fate as Philip's wife; perhaps the quiet love of a mature man makes her happier than his presumptuous, ardent ways. A voice of reason, wisdom, and psychological acuteness, she shows her stepson the horror of his desire for her by telling him, sarcastically, to proceed with overthrowing his father, dragging the corpse of his grandfather out of his grave, and taking his mother to the altar. She implies that the *verlernen* he longs for, the unlearning of family ties—and their legacy—is a crime. But Don Karlos resists the word *müssen* (must). Through his willpower, he believes that he can change anything—"…Karlos is not one to yield to must where he hath power to will!"—and that "it would only cost the overthrow of Spanish laws to be the happiest." However, the spirit of wild defiance cannot triumph over Elisabeth's power of reason. Rebelliousness needs to be controlled and channeled in the right direction to be effective.

The dialogue between Don Karlos and Elisabeth is, to an extent, representative of the shift towards Weimar Classicism: *Sturm und Drang* spirit tempered by reason. Defiance is not allowed to run its wild course, and Elisabeth symbolizes the intellect that restricts a total abandon to this impulse. The Queen encourages the prince to master his heart and become as great as his grandfather, Charles V. Like Posa, she projects idealism onto the Infante, and sees in him the potential to become his best self as the savior of Flanders and future king of Spain, by sublimating his love for her. "Elisabeth has been your earliest love, your second must be Spain." She tells him that it is never too late to be a man, especially one who will be the inheritor of the most powerful monarchy.

When Philip is introduced in Scene VI of Act I, he immediately reveals an awareness of the vulnerability of his love for Elisabeth. Finding the Queen unaccompanied, he banishes the Marchioness Mondecar for not having fulfilled her duty to stay with Elisabeth at all times, and counters his wife's disappointment with an avowal of his love: how can he be more concerned for his throne than for the consort of his heart? As King, he commands the empire on which the sun never sets, but as a man he feels mortality in his love. Elisabeth combats Philip with irony. When she is consoling Mondecar, she asks her husband: "Does force alone restrain your Spanish ladies? Need they stronger safeguard than their virtue?" The misconnection between husband and wife is established from the very beginning; like in Saint-Réal's treatment, they misunderstand one another. Elisabeth's pride and Philip's tyrannical, paranoid, suppressed love keep them alienated from each other. The distance between them increases as the plot gets complicated by the intrigues of those who desire vengeance on the Infante, and thereby implicate the Queen.

Tempered by Elisabeth's reason, Don Karlos sets aside his defiant *verlernen* and, in the next scene, tells the Marquis of Posa that he will try to appeal to Philip's fatherhood to obtain for himself the governorship of Flanders—awarded recently to the Duke of Alba. Inspired by the divine emotion he feels in the presence of Elisabeth, the Infante returns to being Nature's—and Philip's—obedient son. He remarks about his father: "He ne'er hath heard the voice of Nature speak... Then let me try for once, my Roderigo, what power she hath when breathing from my lips." Posa rejoices that the Infante is himself again, yet warns him of how becoming King one day will make him lose sight of Humanity—*Menschheit.* Posa symbolizes love of humanity, tolerance, innovation, and free thought. Don Karlos admires him, and, like Elisabeth, sees in him a true philosopher who cannot be corrupted by gold or courtly honors and power. He asks him to safeguard his virtue when he will become King.

Here is a most revelatory moment in Schiller's depiction of Don Karlos. The Infante requests of Posa: "Nenne mich Du" which, at first glance, means to call him by the informal "you." But this phrase can also be interpreted as "Name me '*You*'" or "*You* name me," implying that Don Karlos longs to be given a new identity—a new name—by Posa. He asks to be reconstructed, to be called into being by the one who sees the ideal version of him. Posa's idealization of his friend turns Don Karlos's every flaw into virtue even when the latter admits that his obsessive thoughts about Elisabeth are not as noble as the Marquis believes. Posa defends his own image of an honorable Don Karlos and declares that even the Infante's mistakes are engendered by virtues: "when thou errest, 'tis my way, amid a hundred virtues, still to find that one to which I may impute thy fall." It is easy to imagine that the Marquis's constant adoration and trust in his friend's perfection are a vital source of emotional and psychological support for the prince. Yet the idealizing mirror that Posa offers Don Karlos is also a weakening instrument, especially when the superlative characteristics that the Infante sees reflected in his friend's eyes are not entirely his own, but a projection of the Marquis's need for a hero to fulfill his mission. The Infante reveals a fundamental dependence on Posa, and feels courageous and hopeful for his future only when attached to him: "Arm-in-arm with thee I dare defy the universal world."

This moment of deconstruction and reconstruction denotes a sense of isolation, an alienation that derives from the characters' blindness to anything but their own perceptions. On the surface, Posa and Don Karlos seem connected in mutual comprehension, but Posa's idealistic projection creates an avatar of the Infante. Animated by his friend's unfaltering trust in his abilities, Don Karlos submits to this exceptional image of himself. However, he can sustain the mirage only when the Marquis is with him, defining him and giving him a name, which also implies that Don Karlos is a construct. And he is a construct not just for Posa, but in a fundamental sense, for his author as for all of his recreators and for history itself. All of the authors who have adapted this story, have seen the Spanish prince as a channel for anti-establishment expression. He is so easily constructible because of the aura of historical mystery surrounding him, yet at the same time he is a valid, identifiable character because history gives him that validity. The fact that the circumstances of his death are not entirely known endows him with an additional layer of immortality: not only does he live on in the annals of history and through fictional adaptations, but biographically, he is a personage without a definitive ending. Don Karlos will always remain open-ended, asking to be fleshed out by the imagination of others, silently demanding a finale of his authors, no matter how fantastical. Thus, "Nenne mich Du" might be the emblematic phrase of this character: the Infante's invitation—in Schiller's words—to both creators and readers/audiences to "name" him beyond his historical identifier Don Carlos—and all of its variants of Dom Carlos, Don Karlos, Don Carlo. Naming him, in this case, does not mean giving him another name, but calling him into being, endowing him with an identity shaped by an envisioned course of events and actions that lead to an ending. This phrase represents the mystery behind the character and Schiller's disclaimer that what the public is reading or seeing can never be the real Don Karlos—history's Don Carlos remains, largely, an unknown.

In a sense, the Marquis of Posa, the only fictional character among the protagonists, symbolizes fiction itself. The Infante's appeal to Posa to be the constructor of yet another of his literary identities gives the impression that Posa stands for an invented author, for a fictional orchestrator of the action. Ultimately, his role is that of a manipulator who uses the personal connections he establishes with both Don Karlos and Philip in the service of his cause of liberating Flanders. Schiller himself, for whom friendship is the highest form of human connection, does not see Posa as a true friend to Don Karlos. Everyone is a means for Posa to fulfill his mission, as Schiller writes in his letters: "Steadfastly, the Marquis follows his great cosmopolitan goals, and everything that happens around him only becomes important to him as it relates to his highest aspirations… Carlos was… merely looked at by him as the single indispensable tool for this purpose, which he pursued fervently, and as such, embraced with the same enthusiasm as that purpose." He follows the love of mankind over personal inclinations and embodies the Enlightenment's growing preoccupation with public issues.

Act II opens with the first of the three pivotal confrontations in which the elevation of the characters to the realm of principles and clashing powers is at its peak. At the center of all three scenes Philip stands as the immutable symbol of political power supported by the church and maintained through the sacrifice of natural laws and humanity. All three encounters determine the fate of the Infante. This first scene is the only private conversation in the play between Philip and Don Karlos. The King represents the distortion of natural laws through political power while Don Karlos is the voice of Nature in his appeal to the father-son bond. In fact, he manages to get the Duke of Alba dismissed on the basis of this bond's impenetrability rooted in the mysteries of sacred Nature—"Mysterien der heiligen Natur"—so that he can be alone with his father. Before sending Alba away, the King reveals his own competitive nature: "I scarce can love those sons who choose more wisely than their fathers." This remark is fascinating in its double meaning: it shows Philip as highly aware of the pacts he must make, often suppressing his true opinions, in order to maintain power. His manifestation of competitiveness is actually an insult to Alba because it comes as a reply to Don Karlos' lack of interest in befriending the Duke: in his thinly-veiled remark, the King admits that the Infante is wise in keeping Alba at a distance. Once the Duke leaves, the Infante fully abandons himself to the role of son, addressing Philip with great emotion: "My father once again!" and inquiring into the reasons why he has been rejected as a son. In the 1787 version, Don Karlos is the melodramatic *Sturm und Drang* hero. In the 1802 version Schiller tempers his outburst by editing his extreme metaphors—his bleeding wounds of the soul, the serpent in the King's breast that gnaws to pieces the sacred instincts (of fatherhood)—and the concluding statement that for twenty-three years the world has called him Philip's son yet the King has never experienced (or learned) that fact. The verb Schiller uses is *erfahren*. Aside from "to experience," *erfahren* can mean "to learn (about something)" which supports the *verlernen* point about parental-filial relationships as both "learnable" and "unlearnable." *Erfahren* here denotes that Philip has never learned about being a father. He constantly expresses his mistrust: he suspects his son of the art of flattery and tells him "Thou art a novice in these arts." As Don Karlos defends himself that, although wild and impulsive, he is not wicked, his father comments sarcastically: "Your heart is pure, I know it, like thy prayers." The mocked purity of prayers here can be interpreted in a double sense: religiously, which implies that the Infante is sinful, or politically, which insinuates that, under his plea for love, Don Karlos is beseeching his father for a role in the monarchy that may grant him future glory. At the Infante's tears, the King recoils and calls him cowardly and degraded. Don Karlos insists that it is Philip's advisors—especially Alba—who have filled his father's heart with mistrust of him and who can never be totally sincere because they work for gold and would never feel a son's love for the aging King. Only this love brings the promise of immortality. With these remarks, the Infante pushes Philip to the realization of his loneliness—representative of the pervasive sense of characters' alienation in all the treatments of the Don Carlos story. Despite his self-control, Philip utters: "I am alone"—"Ich bin allein." As is the case with Philip and Elisabeth, a misunderstanding deriving from rigid perceptions prevents the King from connecting to his son. The Infante pleads to save the father-son relationship or rather to kindle it, because, as it becomes apparent, that relationship has never existed; he begs: "Hate me no more." But Philip instantly shifts the blame to his son whom he believes incapable of giving him the joy of filial love. Don Karlos protests that the King has never involved him in his royal concerns and offers to go to Flanders to control the rebellion in Brabant. An exchange that Schiller eliminated from the 1787 version illuminates the depth of Philip's suspicion and paranoia at losing his throne:

> **Karlos** The King handles his kingdom so secretly in order to surprise his good son to a greater extent on coronation day.
>
> **Philip** Karlos, you speak much of the day when your father will no longer exist.
>
> **Karlos** No, by God! Only of the day when I will be allowed to be a man; and who is to blame when both mean equally much?
>
> **Philip** My son, it is an honorable office you hold—to be an exact minute-hand of my mortality—and, in gratitude, to remind me, your father who gave you life, only of death.

This bitter exchange encompasses the impossibility of any agreement between the two: like Saint-Réal, Schiller keeps them irreconcilable due to doubt and mistrust. The King declares that he will not place the dagger in the hands of his future murderer: he will not give his army to the Infante to lead. Despite his attempt at appealing to his father's affection, Don Karlos cannot fully disguise his own resentment and sarcasm. It simmers under the surface and erupts after Philip's rejection of his request to be sent to Flanders, on the justification that he is sick, insinuating mental rather than physical illness: "Such sick people like you, my son, require good care, and live under the doctor's gaze." In return, Don Karlos wounds his father where it hurts the most: in a comparison of fatherhood with his grandfather, Philip's own father, the Emperor Charles V. Schiller chooses to cut from the 1787 version this dramatic end to the confrontation between the King and the Infante, a moment that fuels the psychological war now openly articulated between father and son. While some of the cuts that Schiller makes from the 1787 version are understandable, at least from the perspective of a temperance of dramatic emotion and the reduction of the play's duration, others are not, especially when they contribute significantly to an even more insightful delineation of the characters, of the relationship between them, and of additional background that accentuates that relationship. Don Karlos seems delirious, alarming Philip, and before he leaves his father, he tells him that he dreamt of the emperor's testament burning on a funeral pyre, which startles Philip. The Infante praises Charles V as a generous man and perfect emperor. He declares how much he lacks as a son compared to what the emperor offered as a father to Philip. The remark is brilliant in its multi-layered connotations: it attacks Philip both in his role as Don Karlos's father and as a son to Charles V. Don Karlos implies, simultaneously, that the emperor was an infinitely more generous father than his own, and that Philip, while taking what his father gave, never equaled Charles's greatness neither as a son nor as a father. With one stroke, Schiller places both Don Karlos and his father in the role of the son who lacks something essential: the Infante lacks the love of Philip who has always lacked the greatness of spirit to understand and emulate Charles V's paternal and politically-inclusive generosity. As Don Karlos exits, Philip's reaction is uncharacteristically emotional like that of a wounded man. He covers his face, strikes his chest, and exclaims: "Too heavy, oh God, is your hand on me—my son—my son—"

Neither Saint-Réal nor Verdi offers this one-on-one duel of words between father and son, although Saint-Réal does describe the psychological misinterpretations that undermine their relationship. Schiller uses this verbal combat to great effect to reveal the political and personal complexities of their double fundamental incompatibility: between father and son as between King and subject. Philip and Don Karlos differ radically in their understanding and manifestation of intimate emotions, political savvy, and mode of dealing with rebellion. The King appears as the personification of tyranny and emotional repression while the Infante, influenced by the Marquis of Posa's idealism, is imbued with enlightened, tolerant views riding on the *Sturm und Drang*, early Romantic spirit of often unrestrained sentiment, and occasionally bordering on delirium. This confrontation is indeed a clash of enemy stars that can only derail and destroy the weaker of the two.

  The second pivotal scene takes place in Act III, Scene X, and represents the confrontation between political power and philosophy: King versus Philosopher—Philip against Posa. It is humanity—*Menschheit*— that becomes the main point of debate between them. The King longs to find a friend who will have the courage to tell him the truth. Briefly, he considers Egmont who, unlike his role in Saint-Réal's *nouvelle*, is only mentioned but never appears in the play. He settles on the enigmatic Marquis of Posa about whom none of his grandees have anything negative to say. He is surprised that the Marquis has never asked for anything in return for his valor in fighting for Spain. The King admires Posa's pride when the latter states that he is happy with simply living by the law as "virtue possesses an intrinsic worth" and has left military service because he shuns the applause of the court. The exchange about laws between Philip and Posa reflects Schiller's double irony at its richest: Philip not only mocks what, for many at his court, is a hypocritical show of the so-called virtue of living by the law, but, perhaps inadvertently, discloses that the law could be used to one's own murderous purposes, especially when one—for instance, the King, himself—is both law and murderer:

> **Posa**   I enjoy the laws.
> **Philip**   The murderer also has this privilege.

Thrilled at the unexpected chance to be alone with the King, Posa begins revealing his philosophy: "I love humanity, and in a monarchy, I dare not love another than myself." There is such depth of implication in this phrase. The Philosopher stands before the King, and declares that a genuine interest in humanity cannot flourish within the tyrannical constraints of a monarchy that, through terror and oppression, reduces the individual to petty, selfish urges spurred on by ambition and by the need to survive no matter the cost to one's integrity and humaneness. At first, the King is opaque to the entire significance of the Marquis's words. While he praises Posa's noble desire to do good for others, he gives him the choice of an official position within his kingdom. He is shocked at the Marquis's statement that there is no position suitable for him. What Philip cannot grasp is that Posa criticizes the very system of his rule as suppressive of humanity and states that he could not spread the King's will when that will does not bring happiness to all mankind. It is an impossibility to reconcile the monarchy's politics with the utopian bliss and freedom of thought that Posa envisions for mankind: the Marquis admits that monarchs themselves would quake with fear if faced with such universal happiness. Posa is aware that he was born too early for the achievement of such a vision. But he never relinquishes his attempts to progress step by step towards his ideal, first by inspiring Don Karlos to embrace the Flemish cause, then by trying to persuade Philip to shift his approach to ruling and avoid spreading a Nero-like reputation throughout the world. The King, too, is a man, yet because everyone regards him as a god, that deification places him in a prison of his own: he cannot trust or relate to his fellow men. As his connection to mankind is distorted by virtue of his isolation, he has, understandably, become narrow-minded and wary. Philip asks the Marquis whether he is a Protestant. When Posa reassures him that their creeds are the same, Philip reacts to the Marquis with increased awe, referring to him as a strange dreamer, promising to forget his rebellious words, warning him of the Inquisition, and granting him unprecedented access to his presence at any time unannounced. During their dialogue, Posa presents the dire situation in Flanders and Brabant where many are burned and massacred for revolting against the imposition of the Inquisition. Philip's repression of freedom of thought and religion in the Low Countries is revealed in the Marquis's words as a crime against humanity that the King justifies as the cost of peace, "a churchyard's peace."

The Marquis's method of persuasion of Philip is similar to his tactic with Don Karlos: he encourages both men to evolve. Posa's phrases to the King are filled with a similar ardor as are his speeches to the Infante, enflamed by his belief in their ability to become truly great which reflects his larger conviction that humankind in general has the capacity to achieve a utopian condition of free thought and universal harmony. Enlightenment and Romantic ideals emanate from his words. He predicts a future age of wisdom in which the monarch's power and his people's welfare walk hand-in-hand, and humanity reigns. He emboldens Philip to lead mankind towards that age, to be an exception among kings and nourish man's liberated thought, individual dignity, and freewill as dictated by Nature, and thereby create a "new earth." Although moved and taken by surprise that a man like Posa actually exists, Philip maintains his skepticism and explains to the Marquis that his idealism stems from not truly knowing the hearts of men as he, the King, does. Nevertheless, Philip promises Posa that he will not be a "Nero" to him and that he can continue to be a *Mensch* in their interactions—but not an advocate of his *Menschheit* ideal. He opens up to the Marquis and reveals his suspicion about the Queen and his son, asking Posa to watch them.

From the 1787 version, Schiller cuts a powerful monologue by Posa in which he replies to the king's skeptical remark that his words are mere sophistries to justify his avoidance of duties to the state. This monologue is a representation of what is happening in Philip's realm: a Spain that no longer suits the individual Spaniard. Posa compares the kingdom to the mantle of a single spirit, a single body, one sole entity whose will fosters homogeneity and submission: "Now genius and virtue blossom only in support of the throne." Appealing to Nature, the Marquis declares that, during these times, he does not know with whom to share his love as he can no longer recognize his genus. A new genus—one might call it *unmenschlich*—has been invented by "crowned mortals" along with novel bonds to Nature, and this genus undermines freedom—the original gift of Nature. Philip's totalitarian rule is causing the distortion of Nature: the mutation of the free man concept and of all that belongs to humanity's natural rights. These references to Nature evoke Rousseau who shifted Enlightenment thinking towards Romanticism by advocating a return to uncorrupted Nature as the solution to human happiness. In the veiled critique of the homogenizing power of institutionalized religion represented by the Inquisition with Philip's collaboration, Posa's philosophy speaks to Rousseau's case for a natural, personal discovery of religion: an individual's self-reliance in the encounter with Nature and a conviction that knowledge of God derives from the self's own observations of Nature and not from imposed doctrine.

However, the enforcer of that imposed doctrine is the most indispensable support for Philip's authority: the Inquisition. As moved as the King feels by Posa and his vision of the world, it would be impossible for him to embrace the novel ideas proposed by the Marquis. The Inquisition is the real power behind the throne, and this is delineated in the third pivotal confrontation: between Philip and the Grand Inquisitor. By this moment, the King is simultaneously affected by Posa's death and angry at discovering that everything the latter has done was to save the Infante's life. Philip admits he loved Posa as a son. The Marquis gave the King a previously-unknown promise of hope and a new dawn, and was for him a first love. There is an intimation here that, being a "first" for Philip in terms of awakening his admiration and love while opening him towards truth and novelty, Posa might have eventually been able to influence the King, had he lived and devoted himself to this friendship. The Marquis's ability to inspire the best self in both Philip and Don Karlos as well as his non-materialistic, apparently disinterested philosophy make his company irresistible. The only one who does not fall completely for the purity of the Marquis's idealism is Elisabeth. In her last encounter with Posa, she esteems his noble endeavor to save the Infante, but she finally understands that the sacrifice he makes for Don Karlos is less disinterested and sublime than he claims: "'tis the love of admiration which has won your heart." These words also reflect her pain and frustration at the prospect of losing Posa. She accuses him of not caring if thousands of hearts should break because of his sacrifice: from those closest to him to the many Flemish hearts he might have saved through his devotion to Flanders. Perhaps Elisabeth—ever the realist and representative of the rational principle—actually distrusts the Infante's capacity to continue Posa's work alone.

The fluctuation of emotions regarding Posa is reflected in the King's extremes of reaction. His sadness turns to fury. After recognizing the Marquis as the first who had inspired him to love, he immediately turns on him and his humanity ideal: "He would have offered me a sacrifice to his new deity—humanity! So on humanity I'll take revenge. And with his puppet I'll at once commence." The puppet is, of course, Don Karlos, and the King is, as will be seen, but a second-level puppeteer, himself a puppet to the master of all puppetry: the Grand Inquisitor. In the encounter with Philip in Act V, Scene X, the old priest is immediately revealed as chief of a secret service: the Santa Casa—the Holy Office—has been keeping files on the Marquis of Posa's entire life including his travels. The Grand Inquisitor admonishes Philip for needing Posa's counsel. He compares him to his father who never sought his advice, to which Philip replies in Schillerian irony: "and he was so much the happier for it." The Inquisitor is angry that, by having Posa murdered, Philip deprived the Inquisition from making a public example of him as a propagator of heretic ideas. He lectures the King and reduces him to a child—even calling him "Philip the Infant"—who has lost his God-given, kingly path by indulging in the need for a mere mortal's friendship. He reminds him that humans are not the equals of an earthly god, and dismisses humanity as a quantifiable tool for power. Such weakness in desiring the company of a human may have brought Philip himself before the Inquisition's tribunal had the Grand Inquisitor not manifested his parental concern and made clear the warning that the King can never act alone. When Philip attempts to justify himself that he is simply a small man the condemning voice of the church accuses him further:

> **Grand Inquisitor**   I see you through. You would escape from us. The Church's heavy chains pressed down upon you; you would be free, and claim your independence.

Independence from the church is an impossible notion for a Spanish monarch. While Philip feebly revolts against the Inquisitor's harshness and calls him a mere priest, eventually he offers his hand in peace and friendship which the latter will accept only "when Philip bends with due humility." In their subsequent brief exchange about the fate of Don Karlos, Schiller illuminates the church's effective method of exalting the King as God-like, but, in reality, distancing him from Nature and humanity. This is reflected in the construction of the text itself. There is a topping of one line by another, of argumentative question and irrefutable counter-argument answer between Philip and the Grand Inquisitor. Finally, the church's perspective has the last overpowering words that condemn even Nature to bend to institutionalized religion:

> **King**   Can you establish some new creed to justify the gruesome murder of one's child?
> **Grand Inquisitor**   To appease eternal justice, God's own son died upon the cross.
> **King**   And you want to spread this lesson throughout all Europe?
> **Grand Inquisitor**   As far as the cross is worshipped.
> **King**   But I am fighting offended Nature. Even above this do you trust yourself to be the judge?
> **Grand Inquisitor**   Before faith no voice of Nature counts…

| **King** | He is my only son—for whom then all I have accumulated? |
| **Grand Inquisitor** | For decay, better than for liberty. |

The King submits and leads the Grand Inquisitor to catch his son by surprise during the Infante's last meeting with Elisabeth in her apartments where Philip hands Don Karlos to the church. Schiller chooses a low-key, subdued ending without the drama of Saint-Réal's poison and vein-cutting death of the Infante, but the personal tragedy runs deep: the moment that Don Karlos realizes he has awakened and become a man—and therefore a real threat—his own father, like Chronos, swallows him up through the sacred jaws of the Inquisition.

Don Karlos was published in June 1787 and premiered in Hamburg on 29 August of that same year to a mixed reception. It was criticized for "its lack of unity and structure," and Christoph Martin Wieland's review in the *Anzeiger des teutschen Merkur* recommended that Schiller go back to the classics and study the rules of Aristotle and Horace. Schiller struggled with the composition and revisions of *Don Karlos* and was never content with the form of the play. The criticisms and his dissatisfaction caused him to rethink his approach to writing tragedy. He stopped writing for the stage for ten years, and began studying and translating Greek dramas as well as writing essays on tragedy and aesthetics. *Don Karlos* became more successful in the nineteenth century: by 1886, it was performed 246 times in Berlin. Like Lessing in his *Nathan der Weise*, Schiller believed that his play should be in verse, but he had to adapt the verses into prose for most theatres. Closer to French Classicism in form, but abundant with progressive ideas in substance, *Don Karlos* clearly reflects the transition stage between

Storm and Stress and Weimar Classicism.

The years between Schiller's original *Don Karlos* of 1787 and his edited *Don Karlos* of 1802 mark the beginning of a critical period in European culture during which this process of rebellion against the rules of Neoclassicism lead not only to Weimar Classicism but also to the Romantic literary movement. Historically, politically, and culturally, the transition is inspired by the spirit of the French Revolution, then dimmed by the disappointment of revolutionary ideals during the Reign of Terror. Schiller had predicted the French Revolution's effects outside France: in 1794 several German states on the left bank of the Rhine were occupied by the French and officially annexed to France in 1797 while Southern German states faced great political pressure. The disappointment with the Revolution could no longer inspire the *Sturm und Drang* abandon to emotion, for it planted seeds of apprehension, especially in observing Napoleon's rise with its wave of totalitarianism and occupations. An initial believer in the French Revolution, Schiller was greatly disillusioned by its aftermath. One of his reactions was to launch a new journal, *Die Horen*, and invite the great writers and philosophers of his day to free the spirit and unite politically-divided intellects. His *Sturm und Drang* emotion-centric dramas evolved through the necessity for a more rational approach to revolutionary idealism, as he perceived how idealism itself could engender fanaticism when taken to an extreme. This might explain several of the edits of *Don Karlos* for the 1802 version. During the interrupted writing and the revision of the play, Schiller's style began to mature and he strove towards a tighter dramatic form. For his later historical plays, such as the *Wallenstein* trilogy (1799) and *Maria Stuart* (1800), he devoted himself to long periods of historical study; also working, from 1789, as professor of history and philosophy at Jena. Yet he continued to take creative liberties with his historically-based plays: *Die Jungfrau von Orleans* (1801)—*The Maid of Orleans*—sets Joan of Arc's death not as a burning at the stake but on the battlefield winning a last victory. In 1794, Schiller befriended Goethe and became his collaborator in the establishment of new literary and cultural standards in Germany. As the main representatives of the Weimar Classicism movement, Schiller and Goethe developed a synthesis of *Sturm und Drang*, pre-Romantic imaginative freedom, Classicism, and the spirit of the Enlightenment. It was not the abandonment to emotion, nature, and imagination that would characterize the Romantic movement of the nineteenth century or the German Romanticism that existed in parallel—and in contrast—to Weimar Classicism. It was an attempt at negotiation between the upheaval of rebellion and the need for temperance in the forces of rebellion. It denoted the importance of clarity of reason when discerning that upheaval's potential for advancing culture as well as its limitations and realistic consequences.

For Schiller, this negotiation began with the mysterious history of Don Carlos. With his interpretation of that history, he created a new type of German historical drama whose distinguishing features are to depict aspects of the national, political and social conflicts of humanity, and to offer characters that represent the principles and forces involved in these conflicts. *Don Karlos* stands at the threshold of cultural transformation, and, in its own development of shifting dramatic focus from its emotional *Sturm und Drang* title character to its agent of enlightened revolution, embodies the crossing over into a new literary territory as into a new epoch.

CHAPTER 4

Giuseppe Verdi: *Don Carlos*
"In un mondo migliore"*

Opera dilates time. The operatic moment places the real-time minute under a magnifying glass to reveal the components of its content. In this dilation, the content of the moment acquires meaning before the next moment arrives, something which, the speed of real time does not often permit. Opera enables contemplation to occur while an action is taking place. By suspending the flow of the action and destabilizing the conventional perception of time, the operatic moment expresses the complex connotations of a situation, diving into the psychological and emotional depths of the participating characters. Operatic language can thus become a musical stream of consciousness that reveals obscured truths.

In its adaptation of theatre, opera serves the dramatic art in a contrastive way precisely through this slowing-down and magnifying of an action. It acts as a musical metatext that highlights psychological, historical, social, and political associations. Since the operatic art form entails a multiplicity of texts—the literary source, the libretto, the musical score, the auditory and visual elements of performance, and the context of

---

* In a better world ("Don Carlo," *Tutti i libretti delle opere di Giuseppe Verdi*, 581).

its creation, influences, and development—it forms a center of intertextuality that simultaneously thrives on and nourishes the work it adapts. In the composer's choice of setting only certain selections from the literary work to music, timing plays a crucial role, both in the duration of the excerpt as in its placement among—and connection to—other chosen excerpts. Opera and theatre can form a partnership that plays with time to explore the moment in its revelatory aura of meanings.

Giuseppe Verdi perceived the possibilities of connection between opera and theatre at a level beyond their auditory and visual artistic expression. Opera could mirror theatre and enhance the drama by revealing the undercurrents of real-time actions. Nineteenth-century grand opera was guided by conventions; the adaptations of literary sources were tailored to suit the audience's taste and to comply with censorship. While, as an established composer with a lucrative career, he was commercially compelled to respect those conventions, Verdi longed for creative transformation. As Saint-Réal and Schiller before him, he frequently found himself in the challenging position of negotiating between his art form's traditions and his urge to introduce novelty to the genre. By the late 1860s, he began to conquer new territory. Opera could be a form of theatre—a theatre in slow motion—and why not attempt to invigorate the emblematic operatic discourse? Why not search for an exploratory musical language that would frame opera as drama in music or musical drama without the loss of either audience-pleasing lyricism or complexity? In Schiller's works, Verdi found the impetus to venture into such new musical territory, specifically with *Don Karlos*. Schiller's words would prove inspiring for the Italian composer in refining the musical and dramatic form of what is now considered one of his most complex works for the lyrical stage, and certainly, his greatest historico-political opera.

Verdi's interest in literary sources adaptable to operatic treatments reflect his admiration for Shakespeare and Victor Hugo, whose works inspired five of his operas—*Macbeth, Otello, Falstaff,* and *Ernani, Rigoletto,* respectively. When the composer encountered Schiller's dramas, he felt an affinity for the subject matter and its power in transmitting progressive ideals. Before even considering *Don Karlos,* Verdi adapted three other Schiller plays: *Die Jungfrau von Orleans, Die Räuber,* and *Kabale und Liebe.* After *I Lombardi alla prima crociata— The Lombards on the First Crusade* (1843)—and *Ernani* (1844) brought him great success, Verdi composed *Giovanna d'Arco* to Temistocle Solera's libretto loosely based on Schiller's *Die Jungfrau von Orleans.* Verdi's *Maid of Orleans* is, like Schiller's *Jungfrau,* not burned at the stake but dies on the field of battle surrounded by soldiers, angels, and demons in a true grand opera finale. The La Scala premiere on 15 February 1845 was moderately successful. For the Rome premiere three months later the libretto had to undergo a major revision due to the Papal censor who objected to the inciting musical portrayal of the French rebelling against foreign forces and singing words like "liberty" and "fatherland." With *Die Raüber,* Verdi decided to avoid professional librettists and appeal to the poetic skills of the play's translator, Count Andrea Maffei, thus *I Masnadieri* was born. The work premiered on 22 July 1847 at Her Majesty's Theatre in London. While acclaimed by the public, it was disliked by critics, in large part due to its weak libretto, since Maffei was a much better translator than librettist. *Kabale und Liebe* was suggested to Verdi by librettist Salvatore Cammarano who adapted it into the libretto for *Luisa Miller.* Considered Verdi's first "bourgeois tragedy," *Luisa*

Miller offered a realistic look at the realm of the private and fueled, as per Gabriele Baldini, "the extraordinary fascination we have for everyday violent crimes." The opera premiered at the San Carlo Opera in Naples on 8 December 1849 and was well received.

The first mention of Schiller's *Don Karlos* as a libretto suggestion for Verdi dates from the summer of 1850 when Alphonse Royer and Gustave Vaëz, his librettists for *Jérusalem*, asked the composer to consider adapting this play. It was not until 1864 that the director of the Paris Opéra, Emile Perrin, approached Verdi with the idea to write for the Opéra, and sent him a libretto by Eugene Scribe, called *Judith*, which the composer turned down. The correspondence continued with other suggestions, like *King Lear* and *Cleopatra*. *Don Karlos* reappeared as a possible subject in July 1865 when the composer was given a scenario for it conceived by Joseph Méry and Camille du Locle. Although hesitant to give up his dream of setting *King Lear* to music, Verdi did at last decide in favor of *Don Karlos*. The first libretto would be in French by Méry and du Locle, followed by one in Italian by Achille de Lauzières.

By the second half of the nineteenth century, Spain had retreated from its Italian territories. It was no longer an intimidating power that presented a territorial threat to the French as they had in Saint-Réal's epoch. During the Second Empire (1852-1870), under Napoleon III, France was experiencing economic growth, and colonial expansion in North Africa and Asia. There was no apparent need for specific political propaganda against Spain and in favor of the French that Verdi would be obligated to incorporate into the opera to please Parisian audiences. Yet while Spain was no longer an incendiary political subject, Louis Prosper

Gachard's historical study, *Don Carlos et Philippe II* (1863) did revive interest in the mysterious relationship between the Infante and his father.

When Verdi began composing *Don Carlos*, the *Scapigliatura* movement (1858-1895) was in development. It included poets, writers, musicians, painters, and sculptors in the mission to reform art. Its adherents, the *scapigliati*, criticized Italian opera as old, stagnant, and provincial, an art form that desperately needed rejuvenation by dispensing with its structural formulae. Verdi had mixed feelings about their ideals. As Arrigo Boito became one of the movement's most ardent advocates, those feelings hinged on a personal offense. Boito had started a promising collaboration with Verdi when he wrote the verses for the latter's cantata *Inno delle nazioni*. The potential for continued collaboration with the respected master of Italian opera was cut short in 1863 with Boito's notorious improvised ode: "Perhaps the man is already born, modest and pure, who will set art erect once more on that altar, befouled like a brothel wall." This, like other incendiary comments made by the young poet on the state of the lyric art could not but affect Verdi personally, and the latter refused for many years to listen to the works of Boito and his *scapigliati* colleagues. Nevertheless, Verdi himself detested old formulae. He wrote to his publisher Ricordi: "I too want the music of the future; that is, I believe in the music of the future, and if I have not been able to write it as I wanted to, the fault is not mine. If I too have befouled the altar, as Boito says, then let him clean it and I will be the first to light a candle there."

While he could not make a radical break with operatic conventions, the established composer embraced the striving towards novelty. In *Don Karlos*, he immediately recognized the dramatic importance of the three pivotal scenes between principles and forces:

Philip's scenes with Don Karlos, Posa, and the Grand Inquisitor. Although he allowed the confrontation between father and son to be eliminated, he remained determined to include the other two encounters. His insistence on adding Philip's scenes with Posa and the Inquisitor proved that he was very willing to create a musical setting for the two dialogues despite the recommendations of his librettists who considered them difficult to adapt into conventional operatic duets. Verdi's letters attest to the fact that it was indeed a challenge to set this material to music, especially the Philip-Posa duet which made him, in his words, "spit out [his] lungs" and acknowledge that "the genre is extremely difficult."

That Verdi is stepping onto so-called Wagnerian territory with *Don Carlos* is apparent from the opening scene of the 1866 original conception of the opera. He quickly introduces the main musical leitmotifs: from the lamentations of the chorus of French woodcutters and their families suffering through war and harsh winter—a musical anguish that will echo in Philip's heartache in his aria "Elle ne m'aime pas"—to the powerful chords representing the Inquisition and other fragments of themes that will be taken up throughout the opera in several variations. This prelude and introduction will constitute the largest passage eliminated for the 1867 premiere in Paris. Its removal is unfortunate because it immediately sets the tone not only in terms of establishing the letimotifs but also in announcing the presence of new elements in Verdi's music; elements whose existence sprouted in earlier operas but that he develops further here, as for instance, an independence from melody and symmetrical structure, and an increased exploration of musical fragmentation and dialogue.

Another obvious departure from nineteenth-century grand opera traditions and the preferences of the Parisian public is the lack of a full-fledged, conventional love duet, particularly between the tenor and soprano protagonists. The chance meeting in the Fontainebleau forest between Elisabeth and Don Carlos in Act I of the original version offers the audience a spontaneous manifestation of love at first sight, although the Infante had seen and fallen in love with Elisabeth (and her portrait) before she'd had her first glimpse of him. It acts as a promise of a love duet exalted by the cannon sounds proclaiming the signing of the peace treaty: "Let us renew the sweet longtime vow that unites us: let us walk together through this life loving each other." But the promise is cut short by the page greeting Elisabeth as Queen. In the Italian translation this greeting is direct and immediate: "Queen, I salute you, wife to King Philip!" In French it is more ceremonial: "Let happiness accompany everywhere the one who will ascend the throne of Spain at the side of Philip the Second." The music of the promised-love duet changes from playful—and infused with a lighthearted nimbleness in the orchestra—to ecstatic to funereal in their realization that their fates have been sealed, determined by political factors as they sing "The fatal hour has struck!" There is a parting of ways with operatic convention in the naturalness with which Verdi treats this initial meeting between Elisabeth and Don Carlos by ignoring the demands for a formal duet.

In the musical conception of the Spanish prince, Verdi introduces new vocal elements. Drawing on the innocent, trusting disposition of Schiller's portrayal of Don Carlos—similar to the gullible personage of Saint-Réal's novel—the composer creates an atypical tenor role or, as Julian Budden describes it, "a new type of tenor in which the simple ardor of the Italian high male voice is tempered by half-lights and subtleties of emotion and mood which will yield a new wealth of musical invention." Thus, from the onset, the open-ended character of the Infante inspires Verdi, if not to institute a completely new category of tenor, but at least to experiment with the tenor role. Perhaps it is also the Hamlet-like indecisive nature of Don Carlos that allows for a finer palette of musical shadings. There are several indications of mental and emotional instability in the Infante. Like Schiller, Verdi and his librettists portray their protagonist as prone to delirium, emotional outbursts, and an inability to act decisively until the end when it is too late. As in the German play, Don Carlos realizes himself that his love is madness. He confesses to Posa: I love with an insane love Elisabeth." During the Act II duet with Elisabeth, he actually faints from too much emotional intensity, and when he awakens, he behaves as if he is under a spell, loses self-control, and embraces the Queen, declaring his love. In the *auto-da-fé* scene, when Don Carlos asks Philip to give him Flanders and Brabant, the latter calls him "insensé" (in Italian "insensato"). As the enraged Infante raises his sword against his father, the chorus exclaims: "l'Infant est en délire"—in Italian, "L'Infante è fuor di sé" ("The Infante is beside himself."). His own friend uses the same excuse to defend him against Eboli who, by disguising herself as Elisabeth, has discovered that Don Carlos loves his stepmother. Posa tells Eboli: "he is delirious, don't believe this madman!" These choices of words in justifying Don Carlos's actions are very similar in both the French and Italian libretti. The underlying idea of the Infante as mad also enables the deconstruction and reconstruction of his identity by Posa. Inside madness there is room for invention. Was it ever possible to truly know the real Don Carlos, especially under the influence of his mental distortions? No, and hence, he could be reinvented over and over again.

This is why Verdi, like Saint-Réal and Schiller, offers hints at madness in his treatment of the character. Don Carlos's historical madness acts as a disclaimer for all three creators, a possible justification for their artistic liberties.

What did Verdi do with the three pivotal scenes of Schiller's play: Philip's confrontations with Don Karlos, Posa, and the Grand Inquisitor? Although, as we have seen, the father-and-son scene was not included, a vestige of it is brought into the Act III *auto-da-fé* scene when Don Carlos asks Philip to send him to Flanders and Brabant: "Sire, it is time that I live." In fact, this is very close to history. The real Infante did request participation in politics but his behavior in meetings was unpredictable and he became a threat to the stability of government. Unfortunately, due to time restrictions, Verdi could not accommodate Schiller's entire dialogue between father and son. But, recognizing the indispensability of the other two key scenes, he paid special attention to them, particularly to the duet between Philip and Posa. He understood that this was more than a dialogue between a king and his subject: it was a philosophical and political confrontation. Verdi's *Disposizione scenica* indicates the following instructions to the bass and baritone of this duet: "It is recommended that the artists pay a lot of attention to this piece, difficult not only musically but also scenically. – The actors must identify well with the two characters who face each other and represent two great principles in the history of humanity." Schiller's *Menschheit* ideal remains the subject of debate between the King and the Philosopher in the opera. This duet proved very challenging to write, and Verdi had to revise it fully or partially three times because the philosophical and political content of its debate required a new kind of musical approach. The challenge also arose from the fact that

Verdi's art was primarily focused on the voice, and here he pushes against the limitations of both conventional musical discourse and his own compositional palette. The duet clearly reflects the composer's striving towards his ideal of a musical dramatic dialogue that tries to break through standard operatic form—"la solita forma"—to come closer to theatre. It is liberated from the characteristic episodic nature of fixed, applause-seeking operatic numbers, and shifts towards dramatic realism. The evolution of this duet throughout its revisions also reflects a change in Verdi's own idealistic view of humanity's capacity to progress. In a letter sent to librettist Piave in April 1848, the composer was animated by the spirit of revolution and hope for Italy's liberation; he wrote: "The hour of liberty has struck. It is the people who want it, and when the people want, there is no absolute power that can resist them." Between 1866 and 1884 that idealism had dwindled. The change is reflected in the composer's modification of focus as he revised the duet: the Posa of the 1867 version confronts the King in more universal, grandiose terms: "What arm has ever stopped humanity's progress?" This is not a literal translation from Schiller but rather an attempt at capturing the essence of faith in humanity's progress that Posa embodies. But in the 1882-1883 revision, Verdi returns to Schiller's words to concentrate less on the Marquis as a walking idealistic principle— although he still remains a symbol of an all-encompassing concern for humanity—and to emphasize his more specific appeal to Philip's conscience about how his merciless treatment of the Flemish will go down in history: "Do you think that by sowing death, you are planting [seeds] for eternity?" This is an almost literal translation of Schiller: "You want to plant [seeds] for all eternity and sow death?" The duet's motivic quality of melody and musical rendering of psychological fragmentation announce Verdi's later style, especially in *Otello*. Posa's revolutionary outbursts break through Philip's suspicious regal mask and lead him to the confession of his private torment. In composing this type of duet, Verdi is exploring a new style. Ultimately, Verdi succeeds in infusing the duet with the quality of a theatrical dialogue which he also does in the Philip-Grand Inquisitor encounter.

The confrontation between monarchy and church is preceded by a very private moment: Philip's aria "Elle ne m'aime pas." Still, in what seems to be the corresponding monologue in Schiller's play from which some phrases are adapted into the libretto literally, Philip admits quite the opposite, that he could never love Elisabeth: "Of a warm fancy she has ever been, who can deny it? I could never love her, yet she has never seemed to miss my love." But while Verdi's Philip expresses his unreciprocated love, his aria embodies the Schillerian Philip's realization of loneliness—"Ich bin allein"—and offers an extended moment for the public to experience the alienation of the almighty monarch. The glimpse into the intimate sorrow of the King makes him more human and sets the stage for his struggle with the Grand Inquisitor in which he questions whether it is natural and right to sacrifice his own son. In Schiller's play this scene takes place after Posa's death, which strengthens the Inquisitor's admonishments since the Marquis was intended to be made an example of and sacrificed for the glory of the church. This part is not included in the opera as the duet occurs before Posa's death, which offers another reason for the Inquisitor's anger: Philip's reluctance to give him the Marquis. The duet is a musical duel between the two forces that rule Spain. Verdi wrote only one other duet for two full basses: for another of his Schiller-based operas, *Luisa Miller*, in which Count Walter and Wurm remember their actions as partners in crime. The bass sound in tragic opera often signifies old age, wisdom, villainy, power, supernatural forces, and Verdi appeals to bass colors even in the orchestra. The orchestral theme that marks the entrance of the Inquisitor employs bassoons, cellos, and basses, resounding low, grave, and menacing like pairs of imposing steps that are echoed by trombones as though the Inquisitor were leaving, with every stride, deep imprints of his religious footprints—and his words. This musical dialogue constitutes another break with convention. Philip's struggle with the nature of fatherhood is overridden by the ascending phrases of the Inquisitor in a topping manner—the Inquisitor's phrases of counter-argument begin a semitone higher than Philip's questioning argument phrases, and end another semitone higher. Consequently, when Philip picks up the Inquisitor's pitch to begin his next phrase, he is already a whole tone higher than the beginning of his previous phrase, and the Inquisitor's following reply starts yet another half-step higher. This musical construction reflects the church pulling the King away from earthly bonds into the sphere of its dogma. The ascending pitch sequence happens over three phrases, symbolizing Trinity, and ending with the mention of Calvary:

Philippe	If I strike the Infante will your hand absolve me?
Grand Inquisitor	The peace of the world is worth the blood of a rebellious son.
Philippe	Can I, a Christian, immolate my son for the world?
Grand Inquisitor	God sacrificed his, to save us all.
Philippe	Can you institute such a severe faith everywhere?
Grand Inquisitor	Wherever the Christian follows the faith of Calvary.

The exchange rises a major third—again signifying the Trinity—in the starting pitches of both Philip and the Inquisitor's phrases. The Inquisitor's voice remains the higher one, establishing the church's supremacy over the monarchy and justifying why the King is allowed to betray Nature's bonds and kill his son. After the mention of Calvary, the systematic musical pitch topping of their debate ends, but the argument regarding Don Carlos's fate continues with one more exchange:

Philippe	Can nature and blood be silent in me?
Grand Inquisitor	Everything bends and is silent when faith speaks.

The incredibly masterful musical conclusion is that, in this last decree, the Inquisitor descends vocally, in a kind of final settlement of the matter, to the King's starting pitch of his phrase before the Trinity-like debate: Philip's indecisive utterance about his son's fate: "That he flee... or that the sword" to which the Inquisitor replies with a question: "Well?" The entire exchange is taken almost literally from Schiller. The focus on the text and on the theatrical structure of the scene is what helps Verdi break with convention to create such a powerful musical dialogue. The result is a perfect example of how music can complement theatre as a metatext that simultaneously reveals the multiple implications of the words. Schiller's dialogue on its own is formidable, but when embedded in an evocative musical structure that offers a multiplicity of supporting connotations, the transmission of its complex messages is remarkable in its multi-level exposure. Supported and enhanced by the music, this act of verbal communication becomes viscerally understandable, at a depth beyond words. The duet ends with the King's bitter realization: "The pride of the King bends before the pride of the priest!" Philip is trapped not only by his own private suspicions but also by the church's power. The Inquisitor's threat—"Oh, King, if I weren't here in this palace today, by the living God, tomorrow you yourself would stand before our supreme tribunal!"—deepens the King's sense of loneliness. The Inquisitor reproaches him for needing the connection to another human being, namely Posa: "Why a man? And by what right do you call yourself King, Sire, if you have equals?" Paying homage to Schiller's elevation of characters to the level of principles, Verdi stays particularly close to the play's text in this duet of clashing powers in which the King is forced to submit to the church.

In opera, alienation can be delineated even more strongly than in an aria when several characters are singing together as in the following scene's quartet between Philip, Posa, Elisabeth, and Eboli. This moment follows Philip's call for help as Elisabeth, accused by him of adultery, has fainted. After Posa and Eboli rush in, Elisabeth revives and lends her voice to the other three, creating a quartet of successive statements of their states of mind. These phrases merge into a sublime music that only serves to heighten the isolation of each character. The King is remorseful and acknowledges Elisabeth's innocence yet even then he is trapped in his inability to connect to her, Posa is obsessed with his idealistic Flanders' mission and decides to sacrifice himself so that Don Carlos can fulfill that mission, Eboli—a slave to her beauty—realizes how much damage she has done, and Elisabeth longs for her mother and even utters the words: "I am in a strange (foreign) land." Besides illustrating that she is a foreigner, the translation of Elisabeth's "Je suis sur la terre étrangère" can also indicate that she feels a stranger on Earth. In either case her alienation—and alienness—is not only psychological, but also literal. The four characters are each expressing their individual states of mind:

> **Philippe** Damned be the vile suspicion! The work of a hateful demon. No! This woman's pride is not the audacious crime.
>
> **Rodrigue** It is time to act. Thunder rumbles in the sky. Let a man die for Spain, bequeathing her a radiant future.
>
> **Eboli** Oh remorse! Bitter sadness! I committed a heinous crime! I betrayed my noble mistress: will my forgiveness come from heaven?
>
> **Elisabeth** Come here, come, my poor mother, see the tears that burn my eyes. I am on foreign land. My sole hope lies in heaven.

They are all strangers. Not in terms of nationality, except for Elisabeth, but in their capability to understand each other as human beings. They are all strangers to each other because they cannot escape their own perceptions and obsessions. This is a scene where the dilation of time characteristic to the operatic art form—the slowing-down of real-time action and blowing-up of emotions as if under a microscope—is at its finest. The blending of the voices is deceptive; it highlights the words in a contrastive manner and thus, lends them even more weight. At that moment there is nothing psychologically harmonious between the four characters; they are each prisoners of their own worlds and they suffer precisely because of their inability to break through the walls of their own—and each other's—prisons.

The quartet is followed by a moment of dramatic realism in which Verdi breaks with convention again: Eboli's confession of adultery to Elisabeth. The inclusion of this moment was hard-fought-for since the topic of adultery constituted an unsuitable subject for the nineteenth century audience of the Paris Opéra. In the 1867 premiere version Eboli confesses only her love for Don Carlos but not her adultery with Philip, which makes Elisabeth appear unreasonable for dismissing the Princess only because she loved the Infante who had spurned her advances. Eboli's full confession is added after the revision of 1882-1883 and it is almost pure theatre as though Verdi is defying both censorship and operatic traditions. Stripped of lyrical melodrama, the mezzo-soprano's utterances are fragmented, un-melodic, almost spoken: "The King... pity... don't curse me!... Yes... seduced... lost... The error I accused you of...I...myself... committed." The aria following the confession, "O don fatal," is Eboli's moment of introspection about the fatal gift of her beauty and its consequences.

Elisabeth's mental and physical prison is depicted to a greater extent in her aria "Toi qui sus le néant"—You who knew the nothingness—made all the more desolate by its setting: the St. Yuste monastery in its austere, cold grandeur, resounding with a variation on the Monk's theme. The aria is as much a prayer to Charles V's spirit for heavenly mercy and meditation on the transcendence of earthly passions as it is an agonizing remembrance of her youth in France and the shattered promise of young love at Fontainebleau, sublimation in favor of Posa's idealistic mission for Don Carlos, and a farewell to life. Elisabeth has attained the spiritual understanding that in Schiller's play appears more as rationality and practical wisdom. This echoes her transformation from a frivolous young girl to a wiser, more realistic woman in Saint-Réal's portrayal.

Intriguingly, the two main characters who are not given dilated moments of interiority in the opera are Don Carlos and Posa. The Infante's sole aria is used as a vehicle for exposition that informs the audience of what has occurred up to that point and of Don Carlos's infatuation with Elisabeth based on her portrait and on a brief glimpse of her. In the recitativo "Fontainebleau… Forêt immense et solitaire"—Fontainebleau, immense and solitary forest—Don Carlos describes how he braved the risk of his father's anger and came to Fontainebleau just to see Elisabeth. His aria "Je l'ai vue et dans son sourire"—I saw her, and in her smile—becomes a romantic reverie of their future together. There is no inner struggle between the public and private Don Carlos as is the case with Philip, Elisabeth, and Eboli. Neither does Verdi depict an internal conflict in Posa's character. Both the Infante and his friend are unidimensional: the former is driven by his obsessive love and the latter by his utopian vision of the world that finds its outlet in his all-engrossing support of the Flemish struggle for religious freedom. Don Carlos's agreement to follow his friend's vision is emotion-based, and his politically-oriented actions are a sparsely-veiled suppression of the hatred he feels towards his father. In Verdi's portrayal Don Carlos is, as in Schiller's, eager to let himself be called into being by Posa, while the latter is the embodiment of a principle. Some have argued that Don Carlos does evolve by the end of the opera. He sublimates his love for Elisabeth to carry on his friend's mission because Posa's death changes him. Even if he is not a political expert, the Infante's decision to embrace the Flemish cause in honor of his friend is not unusual. However, even though, in his last encounter with Elisabeth, Don Carlos assures her of his transformed, chaste love and his decision to fulfill his friend's goals, these declarations seem, as in Saint-Réal's *nouvelle* and in Schiller's play, to be the declamations of an actor. When Posa dies, Don Carlos laments over his corpse and asks: "Oh, my friend, give me your great soul, make me the hero of your new world! Fill my heart with the divine flame or make me a place beside you in the tomb." Even then he is still not convinced. He is still asking to be filled with his friend's belief and inspiring words, which is why it is very difficult to accept that his final statements to Elisabeth are truly his own. Rather, they are learned lines that he clings to because he has no other support in the midst of his thwarted love.

Schiller's understated ending was challenging for grand opera, which required a spectacular, dramatic finale to satisfy its audiences. Yet Verdi rejected the final passionate love duet that du Locle wrote for Don Carlos and Elisabeth. He felt that the Infante's outbursts of "je t'aime" would detract from the sublimity of Schiller's ending and wrote to Perrin: "At a moment like this 'je t'aime, je t'aime'—je ne l'aime pas du tout.'" The composer resisted the convention of thwarted-love melodrama when he demanded that the farewell between stepmother and son remain on the level of sublimation of sexual love to embrace higher ideals. Hence, the drama of the final scene would come from the condemning chorus of the Inquisitors with Philip in an impromptu trial of Don Carlos, alternating accusations of heresy, rebellion, and alienation of the Queen's wifely affections, the order for the Infante's arrest, and the appearance of a solitary Charles V dressed as a monk to pull his grandson into the Monastery of St. Yuste with him. But the deeper the composer delved into Schiller's play through Maffei's translation, the more unsuitable for historical drama this fantastical finale seemed to him. He argued about it with du Locle, thinking it illogical and ridiculous, not to mention historically inaccurate, to bring Charles V on the stage when he had been dead for years. The librettist defended the appearance of the emperor dressed as a monk, especially since Charles' last years were veiled in mystery, just as the death of the Infante. Since Schiller could take liberties with history, he reasoned, why couldn't the libretto of an opera do the same? This ending could also resonate with the beginning in the cut versions: whenever the Fontainebleau scene is eliminated, the first solo singer on the stage would be the monk, which made for a meaningful omen of his reappearance and ultimate revelation that he is, in fact, the emperor. Yet du Locle remained ambiguous about whether the apparition is real or ghostly, which prompted Verdi to refer to the monk/Emperor as a "'half-fantastic character.'" Despite accepting the ending, the composer would continue to dislike both the apparition and the entire concept of a deus-ex-machina finale for this opera.

In bestowing a surreal aura upon the final scene, the ending endows the Infante's brave, last statements with a mythical aura: he is saying what might be expected of legends to say. Throughout the entire opera, Don Carlos appears as a tremulous, occasionally-delirious, indecisive, emotionally-oscillating, and easily-influenced character while Posa is single-minded in his mission and belief that he could mold the Infante into the leader he envisions. The fact that the two do not have the extended moments of the complex interiority afforded to the others can be attributed to their invented existence. As noted before, Posa is a fictional personage while Don Carlos is an open-ended character who is asking to be defined by an invented character, someone who did not actually exist in history. If Posa is an invention, then doesn't Don Carlos's longing to be called into being appeal to someone who stands for fiction itself? Isn't Schiller indicating, as a theatrical wink to his audience, that the Infante's reconstruction and change of course should never be compared to or judged by historical standards because it is based purely on imagination as embodied in the character of Posa? And Verdi captures that wink, particularly through his supernatural finale. Although Don Carlos did exist, his mysterious end, his documented madness, the conflicting reports of Philip's involvement in his death, the myth constructed around him since the sixteenth century, and the commercial need for a romantic hero must have made it stimulating to choose how extensively to fictionalize the character and which historically-documented aspects to add, omit or adjust to the fiction. The element of madness contributes in large part not only to the freedom of interpretation but also to the indefinability of this character. How can an internal conflict be expressed if the traits and drives of the personage are muddled and uncertain? In whatever form this character is portrayed his traits will always be, at least subliminally, regarded with suspicion and skepticism, in part due to the historical fact that he was mentally unstable. Everything in the adaptations could be interpreted as having occurred in his aberrant mind, as many productions throughout the history of the opera's staging have implied. There is always a shadow of doubt cast over any possible realistic portrayal of Don Carlos. This lends freedom to the creative choices that depict his conversion to a hero, a conversion that all our three creators have conveyed, even if Don Carlos never actually gets the chance to act as a hero in Flanders. Therefore, the most suitable end for this mysterious, open-ended character whose fictional heroism lies in sublimation of earthly passion and evolution into a superior being is the end that instantly turns him into a myth, which is neither suicide nor arrest by the Inquisition. It is the end that Verdi gives him: a disappearance at once divinely-sanctioned and triumphant over his enemies, implausible, but more restorative of justice and more affirmative of the power of mythmaking than Saint-Réal's and Schiller's tragic endings.

Don Carlos premiered on 11 March 1867 at the Paris Opéra to an audience that included the Emperor Napoleon III and Empress Eugénie along with members of the court. The reception was not enthusiastic. Critics felt that Verdi had stepped too far beyond his crowd-pleasing lyrical melodramas, but not far enough to establish a new style. Georges Bizet, who admired Verdi's operas, declared himself perplexed by the lack of melody in *Don Carlos*, and by what he considered an attempt at imitating Wagner. In a letter to a friend, Bizet wrote: "'Verdi is no longer Italian. He wants to do Wagner. He no longer has his own shortcomings, nor even one of his good qualities. The fight is over for him… Perhaps the singers will forgive him for this unfortunate attempt… but the audience came to be entertained and I think they won't let him get away with this.'" There were, however, some positive reviews that lauded Verdi's exploration of new musical forms. In *Le Moniteur*, Théophile Gautier declared that "Verdi had undergone a 'conversion' to modern music in 'building' *Don Carlos*, 'his vast and colossal structure.'" Verdi's reaction to being declared a Wagner imitator was characteristically sarcastic, and attested to the fact that he had already been experimenting musically for the past two decades: "'So I am an almost perfect Wagnerite! But if the reviewers had paid a bit of attention they would have recognized that the same intent was there in the *Ernani* trio, the sleepwalking scene of *Macbeth*, and in many other pieces. But the question is not whether *Don Carlos* belongs to some system, but whether the music is good or bad.'" The Italian translation of *Don Carlos* by Achille de Lauzières premiered in Italy on 27 October 1867 at the Teatro Communale di Bologna, titled with the Italianized version of the Infante's name, *Don Carlo*. The first performance in Italian had actually taken place at Covent Garden four months earlier, on June 4, under the musical direction of Sir Michael Costa. In Verdi's absence Costa made several cuts including the first act and the ballet, but for the Italian premiere the edits were restored. Although the opera met with success, as it traveled to other cities—and faced a few changes, such as the Grand Inquisitor to a "Gran Cancelliere" and the Monk/Charles V to a "Solitario," due to the Papal censorship—*Don Carlo* did not become instantly popular with the Italian public.

Religious censorship pursued the Italian composer. His portrayal of the church's tyrannical power in *Don Carlos* must have had profound personal connotations for him as an artist forced to modify his creative choices to please the church. *Don Carlos* aroused the Vatican's indignation and faced the Inquisition of its time. The Supreme Sacred Congregation of the Roman and Universal Inquisition objected to the combination of sacred and profane aspects, the promotion of revolutionary undertakings in Flanders that defy the Catholic church, and the onstage depiction of the Inquisition's procedures, as Gregory Harwood writes: "The tribunal concluded that the opera would excite commotion, resentment, and hatred toward the Inquisition and recommended that performances and reprinting of the work be banned, but that no public prohibition be announced since it would likely draw more attention to the work." The actual verdict stated: "This drama that premiered in Paris at the Imperial Theatre in March 1867 can be called an indigestible, immoral aggregate of the sacred, the profane, the ecclesiastic, the revolutionary, of liberalism, favorable towards the Huguenots… The drama seen on the stage must incite in the spectator, more due to its scenario than its poetry, an indescribable commotion, resentment, and hatred of the Inquisition and its ministers whose well-known purpose is to maintain the purity of the Catholic faith... Its performance and reprinting must be absolutely and rigorously forbidden, but it seems... that a public prohibition would give major importance to its merit."

Despite the aggravation that the censors and the critics caused the composer, these reactions constituted a validation. Without making a radical break with tradition, Verdi was indeed moving farther into new musical territory. He continued to revise *Don Carlos* over a period of almost two decades. It was the revision of 1882-1883 that brought Verdi the closest to Schiller's play. Several of his justifications for the cuts, expressed in his letters, illustrate his concern with the effectiveness of the drama as well as his awareness of historical inaccuracy. In his letter of 15 December 1882, addressed to Nuitter—librettist, translator, and archivist of the Paris Opéra—Verdi declared: "...when you write for the theatre you have to make theatre." And in the letter to his publisher Ricordi of 19 February 1883 he expressed both the need for a tighter theatrical plot and the frustration that the opera does not reflect historical truth: "Don't be too surprised to see the Chorus of Inquisitors removed. It was mere note-spinning. The drama didn't need either those notes or those words... Don Carlos was a fool, a madman, an unpleasant fellow. Elisabeth was never in love with Don Carlos. Posa is an imaginary being who could have never existed under Philip's reign. Philip, who among other things says: 'Garde-toi de mon Inquisitor... Qui me rendra ce mort!' [Beware of my Inquisitor... Who will return this dead man to me!] Philip wasn't as soft-hearted as that. In other words in this drama there is nothing historical..." The revised version was performed in January 1884 at La Scala, but in

December 1886 the Fontainebleau act was re-added and the entire opera performed in Modena, after which it was published as approved by Verdi. *Don Carlos* remains the only Verdian opera to have undergone revisions over such a long period of time, offering possibilities for alternations and rearrangements of material that are used to this day based on musical and directorial preferences. There are "five basic versions" of *Don Carlos*; Budden describes them best: "(1) the original full-length conception of 1866 preceding the cuts made before the first performance; (2) *Don Carlos* as published in 1867 with five acts and ballet; (3) the Naples version of 1872, identical with (2) except for the alterations in the Posa-Philip and final Carlos-Elisabeth duets; (4) the new four-act version without ballet of 1884; and (5) the Modena amalgam of 1886, published by Ricordi as a 'new edition in five acts without ballet.'" Today the opera is performed regularly on the world's opera stages, in the four or five-act version in either French or Italian. Some productions have recreated the original 1866 version before Verdi's cuts for the premiere. Two such notable productions of the uncut French version were staged by Peter Konwitschny at the Wiener Staatsoper in 2008—it included the ballet which is usually omitted—and by Krysztof Warlikowski at the Opéra de Paris in 2017.

As in Schiller's play, the ideological messages transmitted by Verdi's *Don Carlos* are anachronistic. There has been much debate over Verdi's role as a political activist whose works became symbols of nationalism and resistance at the time they premiered. Verdi gained his status as the representative artist of the *Risorgimento* only after the unification. Still, the messages in *Don Carlos* do express a desire for progress and democracy in Italy. While Verdi's operas may not have been instantly considered musical symbols of revolution—a perception that was mythicized and promoted in the early twentieth century—the composer demonstrated patriotism and engagement with the political situation leading to the Italian unification, which would be achieved not long after the premiere of *Don Carlos*. Among all of Verdi's operas, *Don Carlos* is indeed his most political and philosophical work. Without necessarily expressing a conscious intention to create an opera with an ideological content, Verdi did so, mainly as a result of his interest in the personal dramas and psychological states of the characters behind historical actions. In associating history with psychology, he is very similar to Saint-Réal, and in his striving to capture philosophical concepts musically, he pays homage to Schiller. Thus, we can perceive a sequence of influences on the Italian composer that brought political implications in their wake. Saint-Réal opened the path to a perspective of history that highlights both private thought and public—historical—action. Schiller intensified the intimate dramas of the protagonists while infusing the play with philosophical abstractions. And Verdi, for whom personal relationships were at the core of all of his operas, responded to both the psychological and philosophical dimensions added to history in this chain of treatments of the Don Carlos story. Politics and ideology may not have been his primary interests—although opinions differ on this point—yet they became intrinsic to this opera due to his choice to explore the private tragedies of these historical characters.

The personal tragedies that convey the love of freedom and hatred of tyranny, are what appealed to Verdi in Schiller's play. At the core of the artistic endeavors of both composer and playwright lies a fundamental interest in capturing and conveying human experience in its very nature and diverse manifestations, just as Saint-Réal strove to discover and convey the secret of hearts behind historical actions. No matter how powerful and encompassing the historico-political messages of our three creators' works are, these messages always seem to burn brighter from the embers of the personal tragedies that, as the story progresses, take center stage and become the actual dramatic fire of the plot. The tragedies are doubly intertwined: between the human beings at their center and between the historico-political events that are either influenced by or determine the fate of those beings. This evokes Saint-Réal's message that history is created by humans whose motivations are deeply personal and will never be fully known or understood. An author, a playwright, a composer—and a librettist—may take the liberty to fill in the gaps, to paint his or her version of a historical figure's human portrait in an attempt to understand the large-scale events that shaped the world at a specific time. It is an act of speculation, but the personalization of historical events through the creation of very human "actors" anchors history in a dimension that, in turn, enriches the backward look at its sequence of occurrences. It endows this reflective turn with a new understanding due to the additional—albeit often fictionalized— level of connection to timeless human drives and emotions. The immutable historical facts are more easily remembered when one is able to dress them in human psychology than when reading a history textbook. True to his direct source, Schiller, and through Schiller, to the more distant source, Saint-Réal, Verdi's *Don Carlos* turns sixteenth-century Spanish politics inside out, and deconstructs its public, historical representations into a devastating family drama. Through the musical metatext with its capacity to dilate time and magnify emotional and psychological details, Verdi gives a profound and larger-than-life yet viscerally-intimate dimension to the revelation of the secrets of hearts. He transports the story and the protagonists of both *nouvelle* and play to new realms of perception and relatability.

CHAPTER 5
The Sound of Words

The lyric art carries literary works to new realms of perception and relatability through various factors, among which its capacity to dilate time and magnify emotions is intrinsic to the art form. Realistic depiction is sacrificed to moments of amplified emotional expression intensified by the musical metatext. The music and the libretto provide the structure within which the characters' psychological states, situations, and actions are unveiled in heightened spontaneous revelations of complex connotations. And the performers—the singers, the conductor, and the orchestra—transmit this confluence of intertextualities to the extent that their artistic credos, capabilities and limitations, not to mention the negotiation between each other, the interpretative requirements of a stage director, and the physical demands of a production, permit them to convey. Opera is a space of artistic, commercial, and pragmatic collaboration and compromise. Throughout the five centuries of its existence, it has been ruled by various trends: from the reign of the librettist in the late sixteenth century and early seventeenth century to the cult of the singer that culminated in the *castrato* superstardom in the eighteenth century, and the *prima donna* worship and role-tailoring in favor of virtuosic vocal display of the nineteenth century. Today, the focus is placed on theatrical interpretation, and greater significance is given to the visual aspects not only of a production but also of a singer's physical attractiveness, due to increased camera exposure. The last decades have been dominated by the stage director, and productions, promotions, and listings have emphasized that fact, featuring, as an example, David McVicar's *Tosca*, not Puccini's. To a certain extent this has happened with conductors as well; take, for instance, a listing that advertised Nikolaus Harnoncourt's *Don Giovanni*, and relegated Mozart's name to a smaller print. The star system is still active today, and grants prominence to few but intensely-commercialized opera singers, conductors, and stage directors. Nevertheless, when the operatic art form is stripped of the trappings of a production and media, and of the authoritative aura of famous conductors and stage directors, its essence is not altered in the least; it continues to exist as opera. And while the orchestral music and the vocal lines are both fundamental elements that constitute an opera, the singing voice is the definitive mark of what makes a musical work operatic. One can agree with Richard Wagner's statement that "'the oldest, truest, most beautiful organ of music, the origin to which alone our music owes its being, is the human voice.'"

From historical accounts to *nouvelle historique* to play to opera, Don Carlos has been recreated in so many embodiments, but those who call him into being by way of their singing voice add a singular dimension to the depiction of this character. It is a dimension that cuts across specificity of facts and of words to bring Don Carlos to life within a unique system of expressive communication. The operatic language exists in an undefined realm between singing and words. It is a language of emotion that traverses the borders of text and its significations as well as the limitations of historical facts; while using text and history as signposts in its development, it transcends both. It recreates a Don Carlos that is at once historical and beyond history, a character that is at once fictional and beyond fiction. This is, of course, supported by the libretto in opera. The text is the starting point without which the story would not exist, and neither would the music. Aside from vocal ornamentations and the occasional wordless phrase sung on a vowel—usually "ah"—the voice must sing words. Text is a palette that lends the voice its basic colors and sustains its communicative power as it acquires varied nuances from the orchestral music and explodes into a greater range of expressive, emotional colors. The meanings of words and the capacity of music to magnify those meanings are doubly significant in the case of Verdi's *Don Carlos* and its two libretti. As noted, the opera was originally composed to a French libretto written by Joseph Méry and Camille du Locle and then translated into Italian by Achille de Lauzières, while the music remained, for the most part, the same. The nuances of meanings and the musicality inherent to each language of the libretto affect not only singers' interpretations but also orchestral musical colors. Whether the word choices in the translation from French to Italian were based on a particular dramatic vision of the translators, on syllabic constraints, on phonic negotiation between words and the length of phrases, or on the search for words that are *cantabile* (singable), what emerges—even when resisting certain cultural clichés—is that the French libretto conveys more of the intellectual, political aspects of the story while the Italian libretto offers a more emotionally-direct, fatalistic dimension. For instance, the Italian translation of Don Carlos's confession to Posa that he loves Elisabeth: "J'aime d'un amour insensé"—I love with an insane love—is "Amo d'ardente amor…"—I love with an ardent love. The cerebral "insensé"—meaning insane or literally, senseless—that implies an action of the mind and something that does not make sense, is replaced by the passionate "ardent" indicating the predominance of emotion over mental analysis. When Posa reassures the Infante of his loyal heart, there are different connotations in the two libretti. In French, the Marquis' text is: "Pour le sceptre d'or que porte ton père, mon cœur, ô Carlos, ne changerait pas!"—For the golden scepter that your father bears, my heart, oh Carlos, would not change! This implies the political power's capacity to corrupt loyal hearts, while the Italian language in the five-act version "Nell'impero al Re soggetto, tu trovasti un core almen"—In the empire subjected to the King, you found at least one heart—indicates a hint of rebellion in the name of friendship: Posa would defy the empire in the name of his love for the Infante. In the Italian translation, the profound emotional connections of love, friendship, and intimacy take precedence.

The French libretto also seems to convey both pragmatism and idealism: life should be placed in the practical service of goals that transcend personal inclinations. For example, when the Marquis reassures his friend: "ta destinée encor peut être utile et belle"—your destiny can still be useful and beautiful—it becomes clear that usefulness is associated with beauty. In Italian, however, practicality is obscured by personal happiness and "utile" becomes "felice"—happy: "può la tua sorte ancor esser felice e bella"—your fate can still be happy and beautiful. There is also a more mentally-conscious approach to torment in the French libretto, take, for instance, Don Carlos's justification to Elisabeth about why he wants to go to Flanders: "L'air d'Espagne me tue... comme le lourd penser d'une crime"—The air of Spain is killing me... like the heavy thought of a crime. This invokes awareness of possible guilt and the taking of responsibility for adulterous thoughts that may lead to criminal actions, whereas the Italian: "Quest'aura m'è fatale...come il pensier d'una sventura"—This air is fatal to me... like the thought of a misfortune—denotes fatalism, passivity, and a less self-responsible approach. "Crime" has a human author while "misfortune" is an act of fate. The concept of crime appears again in Philip's musings during the quartet with Posa, Eboli, and Elisabeth. Comparing his phrase in French: "La fierté de cette femme n'est pas le crime audacieux!"— The pride of this woman is not the audacious crime!— with the Italian version: "No, non macchiò la fè giurata...Esser infida costei non può!"—"No, she didn't stain the sworn fidelity... she cannot be unfaithful"—the difference in nuance is obvious: pride and the suspicion of crime endow Elisabeth with a colder, more remote aura, while the implication of fidelity to her marriage vows depict her as constant and pure.

The transmission of emotions varies between the two libretti not only because of the subtleties of meaning in word choices, but also due to the phonetics and prosody of the language. The sonorous properties of language—from basic pronunciation to intonation, rhythm, stress, tone—determine the manner in which emotions are expressed at the level of sound, beyond words. Returning to the idea of *cantabile*, the inherent musicality of the language specific to Italian makes it more singable, and, through its direct openness and purity of vowels, more apt to convey spontaneous, unfiltered emotion in singing, while the French demands a certain manipulation in articulation and pronunciation of the words. This is evident, for instance, when comparing the beginning phrases of Philip's aria in French "Elle ne m'aime pas! non! son cœur m'est fermé. Elle ne m'a jamais aimé!"—She doesn't love me! no! her heart is closed to me. She has never loved me!—to the Italian "Ella giammai m'amò! No, quel cor chiuso è a me. Amor per me non ha!"—She has never loved me! No, that heart is closed to me. She has no love for me! The highest note, the climax of the phrase falls, in French, on the vowel "eh" from "Elle," and in Italian, on "oh" from "Amor." When Philip repeats these phrases at the end of the aria, that high note is usually sung *forte*; it symbolizes an eruption of his emotional pain. It is much easier and more natural to sing the high note on the Italian "oh." It is also more theatrically powerful to have this outburst embedded into the word "Amor," although the vocal explosion alone conveys sorrow beyond words. An "eh" becomes more challenging to sing the higher the voice rises, and requires a slight alteration in sound to be more easily produced. Singing in French is an act that calls for more interference with phonetics than in Italian, because it demands an increased mediation between the correct pronunciation and the modification of that pronunciation to produce the optimal singing sound, especially in the higher vocal ranges. Thus, from the onset, the French language entails a more cerebral, aware, controlled approach to singing it, due to this need for phonetic negotiation. As a result of this control in pronunciation, it appears to imbue the singing with an aura of elegance and self-restraint, a combination of etiquette, intellect, and subtle seduction that hints at intimacy but curbs the passions that can lead to or arise from intimacy. One can say that the French libretto of *Don Carlos* radiates the self-mastery and intellectualization of emotions of Saint-Réal's century. The Italian libretto of *Don Carlo* bursts with self-abandonment to emotions and to destiny as if on its melodramatic canvas there were hardly any space for freewill and self-guided conduct. And these perceptions are not a result of culturally-embedded stereotypes about the French and the Italians. They derive from the results of the mental and physical process of pronunciation in operatic singing that is determined by the basic sounds of each language. Some phonetic adjustments are needed in singing in Italian as well—sound alterations are inevitable when singing in the higher ranges no matter how *cantabile* a language—but to a much lesser extent.

Therefore, we can say that the libretto represents so much more than the textual map of the plot. It creates, at the very foundation of opera, a layer of subtle musicality determined by the particular sounds of a language. The libretto contains its own music. With its specific phonetic and prosodic traits, language infuses the vocal production of the singers whose voices, in turn, resonate with the different nuances of musical colors and dynamics of the orchestra. Obviously, these layers of lyrical sounds are also influenced by the conductor's approach and the singers' vocal capabilities as well as the staging in performance. But the particular sounds of language will help light or darken, dilute or concentrate, control or let loose, inflame or cool the range and intensity of musical colors and emotional moods for singers and for audiences. This phenomenon transcends the meanings of words. Yet it is still dependent on words. One can say that the art of opera extracts from words their sonorous essence, and while inevitably connecting to textual signification, it also appeals to the phonetic musicality of language to create the lyric partnership between music and words. Then, of course, style, tradition, and interpretation mold this partnership according to the operatic aesthetics and the cultural milieu of the time.

Sheer vocality can also help disguise the theatrical weak spots or lack of verisimilitude (*invraisemblance*) onstage—in opera *vraisemblance* is in fact inexistent but, when one accepts the conventions of the art form, some operas do offer a somewhat more realistic plot than others—such as the supernatural ending of *Don Carlos* that Verdi detested. Conductor Kamal Khan explains how operatic vocal effects can be used to distract attention from *invraisemblance*: "Verdi solved the problem by giving the *primadonna* her most important high note of the night at the end of the show. Nobody worries about plot; if [Montserrat] Caballé is singing that high B... like she did in Verona, no one thinks of anything else. Intelligent opera composers have always inserted high notes and vocal effects to hide dramaturgical weaknesses. Supreme vocal effects exist where rational theatrical structures fail. A soft ending would make us think too much; but the soprano's final high B has us think about Elisabeth and this feeling that someone alive is pulled away from her when Carlo V takes Don Carlo into the monastery. It's like watching someone's reaction to someone they love getting sucked out of an airplane." An awe-inspiring vocal effect in such a moment of shock instantly cuts through text, logic or realism, and appeals viscerally to emotion, to any human being capable of experiencing the feeling of having a loved one abruptly torn away from them.

If one were to pick the language that facilitated a more direct appeal to emotions in *Don Carlos*, it would be Italian, according to the conductor of the 2017 uncut version at the Opéra National de Paris, Philippe Jordan. He attributes this to the emotionality of the Italian language. But he believes that, even though Don Carlos was composed by the quintessential Italian composer, the opera is at heart a French opera, and this reflects in the music not just the libretto. The French language, Jordan says in a filmed interview, has a fundamental influence on the music as it carries within it the tradition of courtly style, and is much better suited for political, philosophical, and intellectual debates: "French style and prosody are important in *Don Carlos* as well as courtly language. In Italian the text is immediately very emotional. The French version is more intellectual and political; French was the courtly language at the time. For example, the dialogue between the King and Posa is absolutely in the French style. One hears it in the music, especially in the second act: a courtly style with both regal and ritualistic motifs. There are many courtly dance elements, for example, between Posa, Eboli, and Elisabeth."

One interpreter of the opera's hero, however, does not agree. German tenor Jonas Kaufmann feels that *Don Carlos* remains an Italian opera in style, even when sung in French. Nevertheless, he believes that the language does affect the psychology of the character, and of the entire work: to Kaufmann the Infante emerges as softer, more sensitive, more fragile, even more unstable and torn apart when sung in French, as he said to Alain Duault: "I find French to be an unbelievably rich, florid, perhaps more precise language... As singers we have the advantage over actors in [having] the combination of text and music rather than text alone." According to Kaufmann, the five-act version gives an opportunity to explore the madness of the Infante, especially in Warlikowski's production that stages the opening Fontainebleau scene and the first encounter with Elisabeth as though occurring in Don Carlos's mind. This casts immediate doubt about the veracity of this meeting as about the Infante's memory: "Everything that happens in this act, and especially the great love, is super-elevated in the rememberance of Don Carlos; maybe [the encounter] was only a really small tête-à-tête and not a huge love as he imagines." The German tenor believes that love plays an important role in this opera, and that "until the moments when the Church interferes, the political aspect is much more driven by love than we can imagine: even Philip, my father, in his big aria, is actually desperate because he notices that Elisabeth, the woman he married will never love him and has never loved him." Don Carlos experiences love with Posa as well, in Kaufmann's opinion:

> Rodrigo is someone whose love one can't fathom, how far this love goes, if it has erotic aspects that he, of course, suppresses. But, in any case, this love is so unbelievably strong, so unbelievably maniacal, that one wonders what hides behind it. And here is where politics comes into play. Posa is the one who influences everyone: he influences the King, he tries to influence Eboli, of course Elisabeth, and above all, Don Carlos. For me as Don Carlos, Posa is my great role model. I want to be like him, I follow him blindly, and when he says 'go to Flanders' I [want to] do it, and when he says 'overthrow the king,' I try that too… One of the advantages of the early 1867 version is that we have a much longer scene between Posa and Carlo, the vow of eternal loyalty doesn't come right away, there are many moments before that in which one feels how dependent Carlo is on Posa, and this dependence, whether one likes it or not, is also manipulated by Posa who, in the moment of [Don Carlos's] greatest weakness—being in love with his mother—tells him immediately 'now we must speak about Flanders.' This is a trick. I always hope that Posa is true to Carlos, but I also wonder… In the fifth act as Elisabeth and Carlos sensibly part ways forever and are surprised by the Inquisitor and Philip, one wonders who actually organized this meeting. It was Posa who, directly before he died, told Don Carlos: 'tomorrow at Noon your Elisabeth is waiting for you.' There is the question: was this a last-minute political chess move to ensure that everything would lie in ruins, the entire kingdom, the whole succession to the throne that Carlos was meant to have taken over later? (*Alain Duault interview*)

Argentine tenor José Cura also questions Posa's conduct, and brings a universal perspective to the incarceration and death of the historical Don Carlos, affirming that the lack of objectivity is rooted in history itself:

> Uncomfortable people, mainly when their behavior jeopardizes someone else's interests, have always been put aside in one way or another. Whether this quarantine is applied to a political enemy or to a show business, sport, science one... the principle remains the same: calumny to start warming up the plot, then fake proofs to justify the action, then action, whereas action can be anything from physical harm, to moral destruction or, simply, the social discredit that leads to isolation. This is the big, raw picture. If this was Carlo's situation or not, we will never fully know since history is told by human beings and those, regardless of their historical period, are as corruptible, or at least manipulatable, as the ones that lived the original scenario. Whatever the answer is, it is much more fascinating to sail these oily waters when portraying, than simply reproducing sounds and texts without sense: continents without contents...

Even in concert Cura invokes the historical Don Carlos physically: his body language, gestures, and attitude convey a personage trapped in physical and mental challenges, while also childish and eager for affection. He speculates on the protagonists' true personal motivations:

> What better chance for king Phillip II to justify his son's opposition to his political designs than invoking his mental incapacity? Was it really Phillip who condemned his son to ostracism or his Court, afraid that the young man's political posture would end some of their privileges? Was Rodrigo a real friend, or an unsuspected spy who, like a modern double agent, by having his hands on both plates, prevented major casualties?... Was the Inquisitor truly worried by the political connotations of Carlo's behavior, or was he just protecting the Church's 'slice of the cake'? As always with history, we can go on and on questioning ourselves with little chance to have a fully objective answer: History is written by men and men are hardly objective... Manipulating facts is a sine-qua-non tool for domination.

Within the complex network of history, politics, conspiracy, manipulation, and love, language determines how the interplay of these influences is structured and transmitted in performance. As we noted before, French seems to offer a subtler and more controlled exposition of their interaction while, in Italian, personal emotions appear to infiltrate even the more abstract concepts depicted through the dialogues of characters. In an interview with Laurent Ruquier, Kaufmann explains why opera, as an art form that depends on text, is so unique in its relationship to text: "An opera singer has to be capable of conveying the sense of emotion, the phrase without necessarily making the words understandable... Without true emotions, words are empty, unimportant... It is important to find an ideal mix between correct pronunciation and understandability without interrupting the musical phrases... In Italian, direct vowels transmit emotion. [In] French, vowels are a perfect illustration of detail... and give the possibility to express a lot... I seek to be understood always, but understood more in the emotional sense than in the textual one."

For Mexican tenor Ramón Vargas who has sung all versions of *Don Carlos*, Verdi's music was tailored to be a perfect fit for the French language libretto: "The accents and colors were put there in order [for the music] to follow the text in French. The version in Italian is not perfect in this aspect. The translation was not easy and has wrong accents on many of the words. As we know, the French language has a tendency towards having accents on the last syllables of words while Italian has few. So, despite both being Latin languages, this aspect implies a fundamental change, which makes them very different to sing... I find the French language more difficult to sing in, but more helpful in connecting long phrases better; the phrasing is more malleable... Italian is a more direct language, in some sense, harsher, thicker than French, and that [sonority] has a big influence on its interpretation. *Don Carlos* is, at its base, an opera with French colors composed by an Italian." When asked about the impression of more controlled emotions that results from singing in French, Vargas agrees and confirms that this is a characteristic of French music in general: "French music is very difficult to interpret because there is the danger of making it too sweet and excessively mellow. But if you do not give it a certain French flavor that has just enough sweetness to make it elegant, it can be dull. It is like being on the edge of a knife with it: either it is done right, which is a challenge, or it can become kitsch... connected to its language, French music does make the singing seem more controlled. Everything is influenced by language...even symphonic works are affected by the language [in which the composer thinks]..."

In a work based on history, is history restrictive or liberating in the creation of adaptations? On one hand, the fact that a personage existed offers some *vraisemblance*, on the other hand, as we have seen with Saint-Réal, Schiller, and Verdi, the mystery around Don Carlos's life permits and inspires creative freedom. What does this fluidity between history and fiction mean for an operatic singer who is calling Don Carlos into being? According to Vargas, "Don Carlos existed and this adds a certain value to the work, other characters existed... all were breathing, thinking, real human beings... However, we cannot truly know who they were. Still, [history] makes me think, when I interpret my character, what he might have been like in real life. But what matters is that Schiller and Verdi have made him eternal..." Aware of the historical uncertainties and the conflicting political reports about the character he embodies, Vargas believes that these ambiguities open the door to interpretation even wider. He adopts the *Bildungsroman—Bildungsoper—*perspective:

> Personally, I see in Don Carlos an adolescent who gradually evolves into a man because of the adversities he goes through, and above all, because of his friend's death... Don Carlos is a naïve being; his emotions and mistakes come from immaturity and lack of self-confidence, and it is touching to see him so fragile and defenseless... I find that at the end, after Posa's death, he transforms himself into the person that his friend wanted him to be... [Vocally] *Don Carlos* is a trying work for tenor, especially when, as it almost always happens, the first act is cut—without a doubt, my favorite version is the five-act one because it shapes everything better. The popular four-act version is very incomplete. It refers to a love-at-first-sight encounter that no one got to see, and it recalls musical themes that Verdi used only in the [cut] first act that the public never had the chance to hear... Nonetheless, everyone else has an aria more beautiful than the other, but Don Carlos has no aria worthy of a protagonist. Instead, all of his [vocal] interventions are very difficult. Most of the time if you do them well, nothing happens, and if you do not do them well, everyone notices. Despite all of this, I love to interpret him, he is ingenuous and sincere, emotional and impulsive, a beautiful character to explore. All of the music he sings is lovely, from the first act to that wonderful final duet with Elisabeth. *Don Carlos* is a masterpiece.

As regards the supernatural ending of the opera, Vargas believes that it does more than just create an awe-inspiring grand opera finale. It does what all the secrets around the historical story of Don Carlos have done in the many creative endeavors to reveal them: it enriches the imagination. It reminds us that the line between history and fiction is undiscernible where it concerns the Spanish prince, which is not at all foreign to the human experience: "Starting in our childhood we contrive stories about ourselves and about others. We all live in fiction. It is there where we invent ourselves and where we become ourselves."

And fictional invention—be it historical, literary, operatic or personal—brings us back to the text: fiction depends on words. Inevitably, there have been criticisms of overly-textual approaches to opera and of the misconceptions that literary studies of opera engender. However, what such criticism fails to take into consideration is the prosody specific to each language and its cognitive connection to the expression and communication of emotions and psychological states that we have reflected on before. True, intelligibility can be problematic in operatic singing, and one can argue that the performers may be singing in a language that is not their own, therefore their connection to the words' meanings is not intrinsic as is that of a native. Nevertheless, the striving towards diction as close as possible to the spoken language and its innate sounds that every professional singer pursues, implies certain mental intentions and control in articulation and expressivity that unavoidably influence the vocal sound. Even when the volume of sound overpowers the word, the word continues to exist behind it, if only as a mental signifier.

There is another aspect to consider; if one were to look strictly at language apart from genre and historico-cultural context, the words depicting the story of Don Carlos traveled through several layers of linguistic translations and adaptations to become Verdi's opera: Saint-Réal's French interpreted Spanish history, Schiller's German transformed Saint-Réal's depiction, and Verdi's librettists channeled Schiller's play into a French libretto that was then translated into Italian. This process influenced word choices, which, in turn, determined various nuances of meaning, and ultimately impacted musicality. The vast and complex topic of translation, not just linguistic but through cross-medium adaptations, is best left for a separate study, but the mere reference to translation does bring to mind that the subject of Don Carlos continues to remain open-ended just like the historical personage. This can be observed in the adaptations of Schiller's play, in a variety of languages and productions. The living, evolving essence of this story is most evident in Verdi's opera with its ongoing "translations" by stage directors who produce their own visions of the story not only through their particular dramatic concepts, but also by combining various elements from the opera's different versions. Verdi's opera fosters the four-hundred-fifty-year-old mystery of the Spanish prince through its own saga of transformation and the fluidity between its five versions. It refuses to give us a closed-ended, definitive Don Carlos. But then so does history.

APPENDIX

Interview with Ramón Vargas
6 March 2019
(Translation of the original interview
in Spanish, which follows)

In 2018 Mexican tenor Ramón Vargas celebrated thirty-five years of an international operatic career that has spanned a wide range of repertoire and earned him resounding acclaim in the top opera houses of the world. Don Carlos is one of his specialties: he has performed the role in all of Verdi's versions, in French and Italian. Biographical and career information on Ramón Vargas is available at www.ramonvargas.com.

Can you please describe the differences you experience as a singer and an actor between singing the role of Don Carlos in French and in Italian? What impact does each language have on your voice, your mind, your emotions, your body language, your interpretations in general?

Ramón Vargas: Verdi composed *Don Carlos* to be interpreted in French. The accents and colors were put there in order [for the music] to follow the text in French. The version in Italian is not perfect in this aspect. Verdi was always very scrupulous in the creation of his works. The adaptation to Italian was not easy and has wrong accents on many of the words. As we know, the French language has a tendency towards having accents on the last syllables of words while Italian has few. So, despite both being Latin languages, this aspect implies a fundamental change, which makes them very different to sing.

Do you think that "Don Carlos" in French transmits more of the political aspects and the intellectualization of emotions than in Italian?

RV: The story is fundamentally the same, a romantic version, taken from Schiller, of the personage and legend of Don Carlos. Verdi encompassed much in his opera and this invites many readings of it. One could be the power struggle between state and religion, another can be based on the friendship between Don Carlos and his friend, the Marquis of Posa, a third could be the frustrated love of Elisabeth de Valois and Don Carlos in a classic love triangle. As we know true historical facts have been changed. In real life, Don Carlos was not a well-balanced personage. It seems that if he had contact with people who were anti-Philip, it was more out of rebellion than true political desire. Schiller deduces, and Verdi follows him in this idea, that Don Carlos was very tortured by his personal complexes and by the rivalry with his father. His volatile character and his immaturity always lead him to making mistakes, from the first act duet with his beloved Elisabeth. Personally, I see in Don Carlos an adolescent who gradually evolves into a man because of the adversities he goes through, and above all, because of his friend's death... Don Carlos is a naïve being; his emotions and mistakes come from immaturity and lack of self-confidence, and it is touching to see him so fragile and defenseless... I find that at the end, after Posa's death, he transforms himself into the person that his friend wanted him to be.

The music is generally the same, except for the various cuts and variations in the four versions. But the colors of the voice and the dynamics of the interpretation depend on the language in which the opera is sung, and this is not only a consequence of word meaning. The sung language seems to emanate a specific sonorous aura that influences the musical atmosphere of the whole opera. What do you think of that? And what does language mean to you as a singer, as a contributor to the entire musical texture of the opera?

RV: What you say is true, I sang in various operas that have changed languages and the truth is that they take on another tint. *La favorite* by Donizetti becomes *La favorita* in Italian and its color and interpretation is altered by language. I find the French language more difficult to sing in, but more helpful in connecting long phrases better; the phrasing is more malleable when sung in French. Italian is a more direct language, in some sense, harsher, thicker than French, and that [sonority] has a big influence on its interpretation. *Don Carlos* is, at its base, an opera with French colors composed by an Italian.

Following up on the previous question: do you agree that the impression of more controlled passion and emotions when singing in French is a consequence of the language's musicality, of phonetics in general? When one sings in French, it is necessary to negotiate more between pronunciation and the modification of pronunciation to sing than in Italian, which is a more singable language. I imagine that the conscious process of negotiation to articulate in French has to affect, at least on a visceral level, the emotional mosaic of the role. Is that true?

RV: Yes, the two answers are connected. French music is very difficult to interpret because there is the danger of making it too sweet and excessively mellow. But if you do not give it a certain French flavor that has just enough sweetness to make it elegant, it can be dull. It is like being on the edge of a knife with it: either it is done right, which is a challenge, or it can become kitsch. Performing French music well is a challenge. On the other hand, connected to its language, French music does make the singing seem more controlled. Everything is influenced by the language...even symphonic works are affected by the language [in which the composer thinks] ... In *The Gambler*, Dostoevsky said that the French are very gentle in their speech and manners as long as they obtain what they want, but when they do not, a less elegant part of their personality emerges. Italians don't have this problem, they are more straightforward, and this is seen in the music, in a direct way of showing emotions.

Do you believe that singing in French captures the spirit of Schiller's play more than singing in Italian?

RV: Maybe; Schiller thought in German, a language that has another rhythm, very different from French and Italian. Schiller's work is ultimately more intellectual than the opera, similar to when we compare the *Werther* of Goethe to that of Massenet's operatic adaptation; they are opposites: in Goethe's work, Werther is an intellectual, and in Massenet's opera more emotional. German, like Italian, is also a very direct language, but not as emotional. I think that Schiller's work is better viewed separately from the two romance languages that seek to interpret it.

In a historically-based work, do you think that history is restrictive or liberating in the creation of adaptations? Don Carlos is a historical personage who was described as unstable and deformed. The treatments by Saint-Réal, Schiller, and Verdi (with his librettists Méry and du Locle) make him into a tragic hero. The mystery surrounding the historical personage permits creative freedom. What are your thoughts on this combination of history and fiction in Don Carlos?

RV: Starting in our childhood we contrive stories about ourselves and about others. We all live in fiction. It is there where we invent ourselves and where we become ourselves. Don Carlos existed and this adds a certain value to the work, other characters existed... all were breathing, thinking, real human beings... However, we cannot truly know who they were. Still, [history] makes me think, when I interpret my character, what he might have been like in real life. But what matters is that Schiller and Verdi have made him eternal.

You have sung all versions of Don Carlos. Is there one that you prefer, and why?

RV: *Don Carlos* is a trying work for tenor, especially when, as it almost always happens, the first act is cut—without a doubt, my favorite version is the five-act one because it shapes everything better. The popular four-act version is very incomplete. It refers to a love-at-first-sight encounter that no one got to see, and it recalls musical themes that Verdi used only in the [cut] first act that the public never had the chance to hear… Nonetheless, everyone else has an aria more beautiful than the other, but Don Carlos has no aria worthy of a protagonist. Instead, all of his [vocal] interventions are very difficult. Most of the time if you do them well, nothing happens, and if you do not do them well, everyone notices. Despite all of this, I love to interpret him, he is ingenuous and sincere, emotional and impulsive, a beautiful character to explore. All of the music he sings is lovely, from the first act to that wonderful final duet with Elisabeth. *Don Carlos* is a masterpiece.

Entrevista con Ramón Vargas

¿Me puedes describir, por favor, las diferencias que sientes como cantante y actor entre cantar el papel de Don Carlos en francés y cantarlo en italiano? ¿Que impacto tiene cada idioma sobre tu voz tu mente, tus emociones, tu lenguaje corporal, tu interpretación en general?

RV: Verdi compuso Don Carlos para ser interpretada en francés. Los acentos y los colores fueron puestos para seguir el texto en esta lengua. La versión en italiano no es perfecta en ese aspecto. Verdi fue siempre muy escrupuloso en la creación de sus obras. La adaptación al italiano no fue sencilla y tiene errores de acentos en muchas palabras. Como sabemos el francés tiene la tendencia natural de la lengua a acentos agudos (los que van en la última sílaba) y el italiano tiene pocos. Así que a pesar de ser las dos lenguas latinas tienen en ese aspecto un cambio fundamental que las hace diferentes para cantar.

¿Crees que "Don Carlos" en francés comunica mas el aspecto político de la historia y la intelectualización de las emociones que en italiano?

RV: La historia es fundamentalmente la misma, una versión romántica tomada de Schiller sobre la figura y leyenda de Don Carlos. Verdi abarcó mucho en su ópera y por eso se le pueden dan muchas lecturas. Una podría ser la lucha de poder entre el estado y la religión, otra podría basarse en la amistad entre Don Carlos y su amigo el marqués de Posa, una tercera podría ser la historia del amor frustrado entre Isabel de Valois y Don Carlos en el clásico trio amoroso. Como sabemos los hechos históricos verdaderos están cambiados. El verdadero Don Carlos según la historia no era un personaje equilibrado en la vida real. Pero parece que si tenía contacto con gente que no eran simpatizantes con su padre Filippo II, tal vez era más por rebeldía que por verdadero deseo político. Schiller deduce y Verdi lo sigue en la idea de que Don Carlos era una persona muy torturada por sus complejos personales y por la rivalidad con su padre. Su carácter voluble y su inmadurez lo llevan a equivocarse siempre, hasta con su amada Elisabetta se equivoca en el dúo del primer acto. Para mí personalmente veo en Don Carlos a un joven adolescente que se transforma poco a poco en hombre a través de las adversidades que vive y sobre todo por la muerte de su amigo… Don Carlos es ingenuo como ser, sus emociones y sus errores nacen por falta de madurez y por falta de confianza en sí mismo. Te da ternura saberlo tan frágil y tan desprotegido… Yo encuentro que al final después la muerte de Posa, Carlos se transforma en la persona que su amigo quería que fuera.

La música es la misma en general, salvo las varias cortadas y variaciones en las cuatro versiones. Pero los colores de la voz y la dinámica de la interpretación dependen del idioma en cual se canta la opera y esto no es solo una consecuencia del sentido de las palabras. El idioma cantado siembra emanar un aura sonora específica que influencia la atmosfera musical de toda la opera. ¿Qué piensas de esta idea? ¿Y que significa el idioma por ti como cantante y como contribuyente a la entera textura musical de la opera?

RV: Es verdad lo que dices, he cantado varias óperas que han sido cambiadas de lengua y la verdad es que toman otro color. *La favorite* de Donizetti, se vuelve *La favorita* en italiano y su color e interpretaciones se ven alteradas por la lengua. Encuentro la lengua francesa más complicada para cantar, pero ayuda para legar mejor las frases musicales. Se vuelve más maleable el uso de las frases cuando se cantan en francés. El italiano es una lengua más directa y de alguna manera más dura que el francés y eso influye mucho en su interpretación. *Don Carlos* es en su base una opera con tintes franceses escrita por un italiano.

Para seguir la idea anterior: ¿estas de acuerdo que la impresión de pasión y emociones mas controladas cuando se canta en francés es también una consecuencia de la musicalidad del idioma, de fonética en general? Cuando se canta en francés es necesario negociar mas entre la pronunciación y la modificación de la pronunciación para cantar que en italiano que es un idioma mas "cantábile." Me imagino que el proceso de conciencia y negociación en pronunciar en francés tiene que afectar, por lo menos en un modo visceral, el mosaico emocional del papel. ¿Es verdad?

RV: Si, se legan las dos respuestas. La música francesa en general es muy difícil de interpretar porque se corre el peligro de que se pase de dulzona y se vuelva melosa en exceso. Pero si no le pones el sabor francés, es decir ese dulzor que tiene su música y que la vuelve elegante, se puede volver aburrida. Se juega en el filo de navaja, o se hace bien o se vuelve aburrida o hasta kitsch. Hacer bien la música francesa es un reto. Por otra parte, la música francesa, muy legada a su lengua te hace efectivamente tener un canto aparentemente controlado. Todo se influye a través de la lengua que piensa el compositor, porque también en las obras sinfónicas se distingue bien el modo francés del italiano. Decía Dostoievski en su novela *El Jugador* que los franceses son muy gentiles en su modo de hablar y en sus modales mientras están obteniendo lo que quieren, pero en cuanto no lo logran sacan la parte menos elegante de su personalidad. Los italianos no tienen este problema, son más directos y se nota en la música en el modo directo de mostrar las emociones.

¿Crees que cantar en francés captura mejor el espíritu de la obra de Schiller que cantar en italiano?

RV: Tal vez; Schiller piensa en alemán que tiene otro ritmo como lengua, muy diferente al francés y al italiano. Al final la obra de Schiller es más intelectual, como cuando comparamos el Werther original de Goethe y la opera de Massenet; son prácticamente contrarias, en Goethe, Werther es un personaje intelectual y en Massenet emocional. Siendo el alemán una lengua también muy directa como el italiano, pero no es emocional como ésta. Creo que la obra de Schiller está mejor vista de manera separada a las dos lenguas romances que lo buscan interpretar.

¿En una obra basada sobre la historia crees que la historia es restrictiva o libertadora en la creación de las adaptaciones? Don Carlos es un personaje historico que era descrito como inestable y deformado. Las adaptaciones de Saint-Réal, Schiller y Verdi (con sus libretistas Méry y du Locle) lo hacen un héroe trágico. El misterio alrededor del personaje historico permite una cierta libertad en la creatividad. ¿Qué piensas de esta combinación entre historia y ficción en Don Carlos?

RV: Todos o casi todos nos inventamos historias desde niños, sobre nosotros o sobre otros. Vivimos todos en la ficción, ahí nos inventamos y nos volvemos nosotros mismos. Don Carlos existió y eso le da valor a la obra... los personajes existieron... vivos y pensantes. Que haya existido Don Carlo hace que, cuando lo interpreté, pensé en quien pudo haber sido de verdad, pero lo importante es que Schiller y Verdi lo hicieron eterno.

Tu has cantado todas las versiones de "Don Carlos." Hay alguna que te siembra la mas lógica, la mas clara en transmitir el espíritu de Schiller y porque? ¿Hay alguna que es tu favorita?

RV: *Don Carlos* es una obra ingrata para el tenor, sobre todo, como casi siempre sucede, si le quitan el primer acto—sin duda la versión en cinco actos es mi favorita. Le da forma a todo. La popular versión en cuatro actos es muy incompleta. Se habla de un encuentro y de un amor que nadie vio, se toman temas musicales que Verdi utilizó sólo en el primer acto, y que el público no escuchó antes. Todos tienen una aria más hermosa que la otra, pero Don Carlos no tiene una aria digna del protagonista. En cambio, todas sus intervenciones son muy difíciles. En la mayoría de las veces, si lo haces bien, no pasa nada y si no lo haces bien, todos lo notan. A pesar de esto, amo interpretarlo, Don Carlos es ingenuo y sincero, emocional y arrebatado, lindo personaje para explorar. Toda la música que interpreta es hermosa, desde el primer acto, hasta el final de la obra con ese maravilloso dueto con Elisabetta. *Don Carlos* es una obra maestra.

Interview with Kamal Khan
13 March 2019

American conductor and pianist, Kamal Khan has performed with many opera companies around the world including the Metropolitan Opera. As a recitalist and accompanist he has appeared in venues such as Alice Tully Hall, Carnegie Hall and Weill Hall in New York, The Kennedy Center in Washington DC, among numerous others. Additional information on Kamal Khan is available at www.kamalkhan.com.

You have extensive experience working with singers. From your perspective as an accompanist how is singing "Don Carlos" in French different than singing it in Italian?

Kamal Khan: When you've sung it first in Italian, the French feels limiting. The French language is more gathered, you have the mixed vowels, and the lips are much more actively involved in vowel formation. It's a different sonority. The singing has to be more disciplined in the French version... Not to mention, the strength of Verdi's concepts in the French version is extraordinary. But it's very difficult to persuade singers to learn it in French. They always prefer Italian...The French nasal vowels have a slightly veiled resonance, they project less. The overall gentler vowels that exist in French are less penetrating in singing; but people at the time were not singing with a kind of aggressive resonant penetration. All this is taken together with the higher formalism and the structure of the French score, so it's about language with aesthetics, and the cultural traditions of the theatre. In the mid-nineteenth century French vocal style was of a very high caliber; it was the mainstream operatic vocal style.

What are your thoughts on Verdi's revisions of "Don Carlos" in his attempt to bring opera closer to the realism of theatre?

KK: *Don Carlos*, rather like *Forza del destino*, and *Porgy and Bess*, and *Boris Godunov* would have done well today as a series because there is more good material in it than you can digest in one sitting. With the revisions, Verdi made *Don Carlos* more immediate for Italian theatre tastes. He brought greater unity to the four-act version which has a more specific tint, I think, because it starts and ends dark.

Can you comment on the supernatural ending that Verdi disliked so much?

KK: Verdi solved the problem by giving the *primadonna* her most important high note of the night at the end of the show. Nobody worries about plot; if [Montserrat] Caballé is singing that high B… like she did in Verona, no one thinks of anything else. Intelligent opera composers have always inserted high notes and vocal effects to hide dramaturgical weaknesses. Supreme vocal effects exist where rational theatrical structures fail. A soft ending would make us think too much; but the soprano's final high B has us think about Elisabeth and this feeling that someone alive is pulled away from her when Carlos V takes Don Carlos into the monastery. It's like watching someone's reaction to someone they love getting sucked out of an airplane… Even today, there are all of these unsolved mysteries that are such a part of our media: stories where rational explanations do not work. In the high B of the swift ending we get the human reaction which sweeps us away, so we don't have the time to be rational.

José Cura on *Don Carlos*
22 March 2019

Celebrated Argentine tenor José Cura has been performing on international operatic stages for more than twenty-five years. He is also a composer, conductor, and stage director whose productions have been met with critical praise. Known for his intensely-dramatic operatic interpretations, Cura endows Don Carlos with a specific physicality that evokes the historical personage. Detailed information about José Cura is available at www.josecura.com. The following piece responds to questions about interpreting this personage conceived at the intersection of history and fiction.

Uncomfortable people, mainly when their behavior jeopardizes someone else's interests, have always been put aside in one way or another. Whether this quarantine is applied to a political enemy or to a show business, sport, science one, etc., the principle remains the same: calumny to start warming up the plot, then fake proofs to justify the action, then action, whereas action can be anything from physical harm, to moral destruction or, simply, the social discredit that leads to isolation. This is the big, raw picture. If this was Carlo's situation or not, we will never fully know since history is told by human beings and those, regardless of their historical period, are as corruptible, or at least manipulatable, as the ones that lived the original scenario. Whatever the answer is, it is much more fascinating to sail these oily waters when portraying, than simply reproducing sounds and texts without sense: continents without contents...

Now, if to his [apparent] political incorrectness, we add his physical and psychological rarity in a period of the humanity where these things were regarded as a devil's mark... What would have happened to guys like Van Gogh, Toulouse-Lautrec, Forbes, Nash, Hawkins, to mention only a handful, if they had lived in those years? What better chance for king Phillip II to justify his son's opposition to his political designs, than invoking his mental incapacity? Was it really Phillip who condemned his son to ostracism or his Court, afraid that the young man's political posture would end with some of their privileges? Was Rodrigo a real friend, or an unsuspected spy who, like a modern double agent, by having his hands on both plates, prevented major casualties? Was there a true love between Carlo and Elisabetta, or simply the reassuring complicity of two kids being squeezed by the same unbearable weight? Was the Inquisitor truly worried by the political connotations of Carlo's behavior, or was he just protecting the Church's "slice of the cake"? As always with history, we can go on and on questioning ourselves with little chance to have a fully objective answer: History is written by men and men are hardly objective.

You say: "This personage is on one hand historical, and on the other a myth, a fiction because no one truly knows the entire truth about his end" and I ask: Do we know the entire truth of Pearl Harbor's attack almost 80 years after? Too far? Carlo's drama is even farther... Do we know the entire truth about September 11, 2001? That one is not so far... You add: "... mystery opens the door to fiction while Carlo still remains historical" and I ask: is there anyone upon whom history and fiction have created a more powerful (useful?) cocktail than Jesus Christ? I truly believe He would be disgusted with what most of His heritage has become. Manipulating facts is a sine-qua-non tool for domination.

In conclusion, actors will never fully know the historical truth of the characters they portray when they are historical, therefore, reading as much as possible, then processing the data in order to create an interpretation, is as far as we can go. Some people may disagree with our vision on a certain historical-persona, but they will do it based on the same incomplete (or manipulated) information we have used to create such vision, so take a deep breath and move on!

José Cura, Madrid, March 22, 2019

BIBLIOGRAPHY

Abbate, Carolyn, and Roger Parker. *A History of Opera.* New York: W.W. Norton, 2015.

Abbiati, Franco. *Giuseppe Verdi.* 4 Volumes. Ricordi, 1959.

Alfieri, Vittorio. *Filippo.* 1783. Revisione di Claudio Paganelli. *Liber Liber: Progetto Manuzio,* 2000. www.liberliber.it/mediateca/libri/a/alfieri/filippo/pdf/filipp_p.pdf. 17 September 2018.

Alvar Ezquerra, Alfredo. *La leyenda negra.* Kindle edition. Ediciones Akal, 1997.

Atti dei congressi internazionali di studi Verdiani. 3 volumes. Istituto nazionale di studi verdiani, 1969, 1972, 1974.

Bainton, Roland H. *Women of the Reformation in France and England.* Minneapolis: Ausburg Publishing House, 1973.

Bakos, Adrianna E. "'Qui Nescit Dissimulare, Nescit Regnare': Louis XI and Raison D'etat During the Reign of Louis XIII." *Journal of the History of Ideas,* vol. 52, no. 3, 1991, pp. 399–416. *JSTOR,* www.jstor.org/stable/2710044. 10 April 2019.

Baldini, Gabriele, *The Story of Giuseppe Verdi.* Translated by Roger Parker. Cambridge University Press, 1980.

Beiser, Frederick. *Schiller as Philosopher: A Re-Examination.* Clarendon Press, 2005.

Benjamin, Walter. "The Task of the Translator." *Selected Writings Volume 1 1913-1926.* Edited by Marcus Bullock and Michael W. Jennings. The Belknap Press of Harvard University Press, 1996. Fifth printing, 2002, pp. 253-263.

Berger, William. *Verdi with a Vengeance.* Vintage Books, 2000.

Brantôme, Pierre de Bourdeille, seigneur de. "Philippe II Roy d'Espagne." *Memoires de messire Pierre de Bourdeille, seigneur de Brantôme.* Contenans les vies des hommes illustres & grands capitaines estrangers de son temps, pp. 384-409. Leyden: Sambix, 1665. *Internet Archive.* archive.org/stream/ned-kbn-all-00002750-001#page/n406. 17 September 2018.

---. "Elizabeth de France." *Vies des dames illustres françoises et étrangères.* Nouvelle édition, pp. 156-177. Paris: Garnier frères, 1868. *Internet Archive.* archive.org/stream/bub_gb_7GtI_QDN850C#page/n205. 17 September 2018.

Bruford, W.H. *Theatre, Drama, and Audience in Goethe's Germany.* Routledge & Kegan Paul LTD., 1957.

Budden, Julian. *The Operas of Verdi: Volume 3: From Don Carlos to Falstaff.* Oxford University Press, 2002.

Cammarano, Salvatore. "Luisa Miller." *Tutti i libretti delle opere di Giuseppe Verdi*, pp. 1555-1642. *Internet Archive.* archive.org/details/TuttiILibretti DelleOpereDiGiuseppeVerdi. 15 September 2018.

Carlson, Marvin. *Goethe and the Weimar Theatre.* Cornell University Press, 1978.

---. *The Haunted Stage.* Ann Arbor: The University of Michigan Press, 2001.

Conati, Marcello and Mario Medici eds. *The Verdi-Boito Correspondence.* Translated by William Weaver. The University of Chicago Press, 1994.

Cormon, Eugène. *Phillipe II Roi d'Espagne.* Huesca, 1634. Michel Levy Frères, 1846. *Google Books.* play.google.com/books/reader?id=9fFRAAAAcAAJ& pg=GBS.PP1. 14 September 2018.

Cuénin, Micheline, ed. *Histoire de la Princesse de Montpensier sous le règne de Charles IXème Roi de France; Histoire de la Comtesse de Tende by Madame de Lafayette.* Genève: Droz, 1979.

Cura, José. Personal interview. 22 March 2019.

Dahlstrom, Daniel. "Play and Irony: Schiller and Schlegel on the Liberating Prospects of Aesthetics." *The History of Continental Philosophy, Volume 1.* Edited by Alan Schrift. University of Chicago Press, 2011.

Deloffre, Frederic. La nouvelle en France à l'age classique. Didier, 1968.

Disposizione scenica per l'opera Don Carlo di Giuseppe Verdi compilata regolata secondo la mise-en-scene del Teatro Imperiale di Opera di Parigi (1st ed. Milan, 1867, 3rd ed. 1884)

Duault, Alain. "Don Carlos à l'Opéra de Paris: rencontre avec Jonas Kaufmann." *YouTube*, uploaded by Opera Online, 12 October 2017, youtu.be/7Je-Ya4sMSI1. 14 March 2019.

Du Locle, Camille and Joseph Méry. Don Carlos: opéra en cinq actes / paroles de Méry et *Camille du Locle ; musique de G. Verdi.* Paris: M. Levy, L. Escudier, 1867. *UR Research at the University of Rochester.* hdl.handle.net/1802/14328. 15 September 2018

---. *Don Carlo: Grande-opéra in cinque atti*. Translated by Achille de Lauzières and Angelo Zanardini. *Opera Today*, 2006. www.operatoday.com/content/2006/10/verdi_don_carlo_4.php.15 September 2018.

Dulong, Gustave. *L'abbé de Saint-Réal; étude sur les rapports de l'histoire et du roman au 17e Siècle*. Paris: Champion, 1921. *Internet Archive*. archive.org/details/labbdesaintr02dulouoft. 16 September 2018.

Enciso, Diego Jiménez de. "El Principe Don Carlos." 1634. *Biblioteca virtual Miguel de Cervantes*, 2012. www.cervantesvirtual.com/obra/el-principe-don-carlos-2/. 17 September 2018.

Fabre, Jean. *L'art de l'analyse de la Princesse de Clèves*. Editions Ophrys, 1970.

Finger, Ellis. "Schiller's Concept of the Sublime and its Pertinence to 'Don Carlos's and 'Maria Stuart.'" *The Journal of English and Germanic Philology*, vol. 79, no, 2, April 1980. www.jstor.org/stable/27708639. 11 January 2019.

Freer, Martha Walker. *Jeanne d'Albret, Queen of Navarre, 1528-1572*. London: Hurst and Blackett. *Internet Archive*. archive.org/details/lifeofjeannedalb00free/page/n7 . 22 November 2018.

Gachard, Louis Prosper. *Don Carlos et Philippe II*. Deuxième édition. Paris: Michel Lévy frères, 1867. *Internet Archive*. archive.org/stream/doncarloset phil00gachgoog?ref=ol#page/n11. 18 September 2018.

Goethe, Johann Wolfgang von. "Egmont." Translated by Anna Swanwick, 2008. *Project Gutenberg*. www.gutenberg.org/files/1945/1945-h/1945-h.htm. 12 December 2018.

Goodwin, Robert. *Spain: The Centre of the World 1519 – 1682*. Bloomsbury, 2015.

Gossett, Philip. "Giuseppe Verdi and the Italian Risorgimento." *Studia Musicologica*, vol. 52, no. 1/4, 2011, pp. 241–257. *JSTOR*, www.jstor.org/stable/43289762.

Gould, Kevin. *Catholic Activism in South-West France, 1540-1570*. Routledge, 2006.

Grande, Nathalie. "Enjeux esthétiques et idéologiques de la representation historique dans *Les Amours des Grands Hommes* de Madame de Villedieu (1671)," *Fiction et histoire, France-Italie*, dir. A. Peyronie, *Atlantide*, no.3, 2015, atlantide.univ-nantes.fr/Representation-historique-enjeux. 19 November 2018.

Günther, Ursula. "La genèse de Don Carlos, opéra en 5 Actes de Giuseppe Verdi, representé pour la première fois à Paris le 11 mars 1867." *Revue de Musicologie* LVIII. Paris, 1972.

Hammer, Stephanie Barbé. *Schiller's Wound: The Theatre of Trauma from Crisis to Commodity.* Wayne State University Press, 2001.

Hammill, Graham and Julia Reinhard Lupton, eds. *Political Theology and Early Modernity.* University of Chicago Press, 2012.

Harwood, Gregory W. *Giuseppe Verdi: A Research and Information Guide*, second edition. Routledge, 2012.

Hegel, Georg Wilhelm Friedrich. *Aesthetics: Lectures on Fine Art.* Translated by T.M. Knox. Oxford University Press, 1975.

Heine, Heinrich. "The Romantic School." Translated by Helen Mustard. *The Romantic School and Other Essays.* The Continuum Publishing Company, 2002.

Hillgarth, Jocelyn N. *The Mirror of Spain 1500-1700: The Formation of a Myth (Histories, Languages, and Cultures of the Spanish and Portuguese Worlds).* University of Michigan Press, 2000.

Höink, Dominik. "Das Zensurverfahren Gegen Giuseppe Verdis 'Don Carlo' Vor Der Römischen Inquisition." *Die Musikforschung*, vol. 60, no. 4, 2007, pp. 362–377. *JSTOR*, www.jstor.org/stable/41126225. 21 January 2019.

Horton, Scott. "'What Is, and To What End Do We Study Universal History.'" *Harper's Magazine*, 23 July 2007. harpers.org/blog/2007/07/what-is-and-to-what-end-do-we-study-history/ 11 April 2019.

Hume, Martin Andrew Sharp. *Philip II of Spain.* Original publication 1897. London: Macmillan and co., limited; New York: the Macmillan company, 1906. *Internet Archive*.archive.org/details/philipiispain01humegoog/page/n8. 23 November 2018.

Jackson, Jennifer. "Don Carlos: Narrative transformation in the works of Abbé de Saint-Réal, Friedrich Schiller and Giuseppe Verdi." *Études sur l'opéra français du XIXe siècle,* vol. VIII. Musik-Edition Lucie Galland, 2008.

Jakobson, Roman. "On Linguistic Aspects of Translation," *On Translation*, Harvard University Press, 1959, pp 233-239, web.stanford.edu/~eckert/PDF/jakobson.pdf. 10 February 2019.

"Jonas Kaufmann - On n'est pas couché 7 octobre 2017." *YouTube*, uploaded by On n'est pas couché, 7 October 2017, youtu.be/MiUKhky2YA8. 1 February 2019.

Jones, William. "Friedrich Schiller and His Friends." *Fidelio*, vol 14, no. 1-2, Spring-Summer 2005. *schillerinstitute.com* pp. 54-79. 12 January 2019.

Kale, Steven. *French Salons: High Society and Political Sociability from the Old Regime to the Revolution of 1848*. Johns Hopkins University Press, 2004.

Kamen, Henry. *Philip of Spain*. Yale University Press, 1999.

Kotnik, Vlado. *Opera as Anthropology*. Cambridge Scholars Publishing, 2016.

"Krzysztof Warlikowski à propos de *Don Carlos*." *YouTube*, uploaded by Opéra national de Paris, 25 January 2017. youtu.be/bVaoVpHrSa8. 5 February 2019.

La Fayette, Madame de. *La princesse de Clèves*. Kindle edition. Éditions eBooks France: May, 2010. 20 December 2018.

Lafond Jean. "L'imaginaire de la conjuration dans la littérature française du XVIIe siècle." *Complots et conjurations dans l'Europe moderne. Actes du colloque international organisé à Rome, 30 septembre-2 octobre 1993*. Rome: École Française de Rome, 1996. pp. 117-135. www.persee.fr/doc/efr_0223-5099_1996_act_220_1_4979. 23 November 2018.

Lessing, Gotthold Ephraim. "Hamburgische Dramaturgie." *Project Gutenberg*. www.gutenberg.org/ebooks/10055. 20 January 2019.

Lieder, Frederick W.C. "The Don Carlos Theme in Literature." *The Journal of English and Germanic Philology*, vol.9, no.4, 1910, pp. 483-498. www.jstor.org/stable/27700054. 15 June 2018.

Lukács, Georg. *The Historical Novel*, translated by Hannah and Stanley Mitchell. Lincoln: University of Nebraska Press, 1983.

Maffei, Andrea. "I masnadieri." *Tutti i libretti delle opere di Giuseppe Verdi*, pp. 1708-1772. *Internet Archive*. archive.org/details/TuttiILibrettiDelleOpereDiGiuseppeVerdi. 15 September 2018.

Majid, Asifa. "Current Emotion Research in the Language Sciences." *Sage Journals: Emotion Review*, 17 July 2012, doi.org/10.1177/1754073912445827. 19 March 2019.

Mansau, Andrée. *Saint Réal et l'humanisme cosmopolite*. Champion, 1976.

Martinenche, Ernest. *Histoire de l'influence espagnole sur la littérature française. L'Espagne et le romantisme français*. Hachette, 1922. *Internet Archive*. archive.org/details/histoiredelinflu00martuoft/page/n5. 19 November 2018.

Mendelsohn, Gerald A. "Verdi the Man and Verdi the Dramatist." *19th-Century Music*, vol. 2, no. 2, 1978, pp.110-142. *JSTOR*, www.jstor.org/stable/746308. 15 June 2018.

---. "Verdi the Man and Verdi the Dramatist (II)." *19th-Century Music*, vol. 2, no. 3, 1979, pp. 214-230. *JSTOR*, www.jstor.org/stable/3519798. 15 June 2018.

Otway, Thomas. *Don Carlos, Prince of Spain*. London: Stage Door, 2017.

Parker, Geoffrey. *Philip II*. Chicago: Open Court, 2002.

Parker, Roger. "Philippe and Posa Act II: The Shock of the New." *Cambridge Opera Journal*, vol. 14, no. 1/2, 2002, pp. 133-147. *JSTOR*, www.jstor.org/stable/3878287. 15 June 2018.

Pérez, Joseph. *La légende noire de l'Espagne*. Fayard, 2009.

"Philippe Jordan à propos de *Don Carlos*." *YouTube*, uploaded by Opéra national de Paris, 20 September 2017. youtu.be/Mznkad1uvP8. 5 February 2019.

Phillips-Matz, Mary Jane. *Verdi: A Biography*. New edition. Oxford University Press, 1996.

Piave, Francesco Maria. "I due Foscari." *Tutti i libretti delle opere di Giuseppe Verdi*, pp. 798-869. archive.org/details/TuttiILibrettiDelleOpereDiGiuseppeVerdi. 15 September 2018.

---. "La forza del destino." *Tutti i libretti delle opere di Giuseppe Verdi*, pp. 1093-1233.

---. "Simon Boccanegra." *Tutti i libretti delle opere di Giuseppe Verdi*, pp. 2060-2171.

Porter, Andrew. "The Making of 'Don Carlos'." *Proceedings of the Royal Musical Association*, vol. 98, 1971, pp. 73–88. *JSTOR*, www.jstor.org/stable/766106. 14 February 2019.

Powell, Philip Wayne. *Tree of Hate*. University of New Mexico Press, 2008.

Pratt, Mary Louise. "Arts of the Contact Zone." *Profession*, 1991, pp. 33–40. *JSTOR*, www.jstor.org/stable/25595469. 1 April 2019.

Robinson, Paul. "A Deconstructive Postscript: Reading Libretti and Misreading Opera." *Reading Opera*, edited by Arthur Groos and Roger Parker, Princeton University Press, 1988, pp. 328–346. *JSTOR*, www.jstor.org/stable/j.ctt7ztx1g.17. 1 February 2019.

---. "Realpolitik: Giuseppe Verdi's Don Carlo." *Opera & Ideas from Mozart to Strauss*, Cornell University Press, 1986.

Rosen, David. "'Don Carlos's as 'Bildungsoper:' Carlos's Last Act." *Cambridge Opera Journal*, vol. 14, no. 1/2, 2002, pp. 109-131. *JSTOR*, www.jstor.org/stable/3878286. 15 June 2018.

Royer, Alphonse and Gustave Vaëz. "Gerusalemme." Translated by Calisto Bassi. *Tutti i libretti delle opere di Giuseppe Verdi*, pp. 1234-1304. archive.org/details/TuttiILibrettiDelleOpereDiGiuseppeVerdi. 15 September 2018.

---. "Jérusalem." *Tutti i libretti delle opere di Giuseppe Verdi*, pp. 1425-1497.

Saint-Réal, César Vichard de. *Conjuration des espagnols contre Venise, en 1618*. Paris: L'Imprimerie De Monsieur, 1781. *Internet Archive*. archive.org/stream/ conjurationdeses00sain#page/n7. 18 September 2018.

---. *De l'usage de l'histoire*. Paris: Etienne Michallet Marchand Librarie, 1671. *Google Books*. play.google.com/books/reader?id=3HwKPJykRKwC&hl=en &pg=GBS.PP7. 18 November 2018.

---. *Dom Carlos*. Livre de Poche, 2004.

---. *Don Carlos, Prince of Spain a tragedy: as it was acted at the Duke's theatre / written by Tho. Otway. (1695)*. EEBO Editions, ProQuest 2010.

Schiller, Friedrich. *Briefe über Don Carlos*. Amazon Digital Services, 2011.

---. *Dom Karlos Infant von Spanien*. Göschen, Leipzig,1787. *Deutsches Textarchiv*. www.deutschestextarchiv.de / book / show / schiller_domkarlos_ 1787. 14 September 2018.

---. *Don Karlos Infant von Spanien*. Leipzig: Göschen, 1802. *Google Books*. books.google.de/books?id=uqb04B7XArAC. 14 September 2018.

---. "Don Carlos." Translated by R.D. Boylan, *Complete Poetical Works and Plays of Friedrich Schiller*. Delphi Classics, 2013.

---. "Fiesco's Conspiracy at Genoa." Translated by C.J. Hempel. Delphi Classics, 2013.

---. "Intrigue and Love." Translated by Alexander Fraser Tytler. Delphi Classics, 2013.

---. "Mary Stuart." Translated by Joseph Mellish. Delphi Classics, 2013.

---. *On the Aesthetic Education of Man*. Translated by Reginald Snell. Dover Publications, 2012.

---. "The Maid of Orleans." Translated by Ana Swanwick. Delphi Classics, 2013.

---. "The Robbers." Translated by Alexander Fraser Tytler. Delphi Classics, 2013.

---. "Turandot." Translated by Sabilla Novello. Delphi Classics, 2013.

---. "Wallenstein Trilogy." Translated by Samuel Taylor Coleridge and James Churchill. Delphi Classics, 2013.

---. "What Is, and To What End do We Study Universal History." Translated by Caroline Stephan and Robert Trout. Poet of Freedom, Volume II. The Schiller Institute. archive.schillerinstitute.com / transl / Schiller_essays / universal_ history.pdf. 10 April 2019.

---. "Wilhelm Tell." Translated by Theodore Martin. Delphi Classics, 2013.

Scribe, Augustin Eugene and Charles Duveyrier. "Les vêpres siciliennes." *Tutti i libretti delle opere di Giuseppe Verdi*, pp. 2520-2636.

---. "I vespri siciliani." Translated by Arnaldo Fusinato. *Tutti i libretti delle opere di Giuseppe Verdi*, pp. 2407-2519. Schmidgall, Gary. Literature as Opera. Oxford University Press, 1977.

Sharpe, Lesley. Friedrich Schiller: Drama, Thought and Politics. Cambridge University Press, 1991.

Solera, Temistocle. "Giovanna d'Arco." *Tutti i libretti delle opere di Giuseppe Verdi*, pp. 1376-1424.

Spingarn, J.E., ed. *Goethe's Literary Essays*. Harcourt, Brace, and Company, 1921.

Swiggett, Glen Levin. "The Message in Friedrich Schiller's Life." *The Sewanee Review*, vol. 13, no. 4 (Oct., 1905), pp. 413-443. www.jstor.org/stable/27530716. 10 January 2019.

Vargas, Ramón. Personal interview. 6 March 2019.

Villalon, L. J. Andrew. "Putting Don Carlos Together Again: Treatment of a Head Injury in Sixteenth-Century Spain." *The Sixteenth Century Journal*, vol. 26, no.2, 1995, pp. 347-365. www.jstor.org/stable/2542795. 15 June 2018.

Villedieu, Madame de. *Annales galantes*. Claude Barbin, 1670. Slatkine Reprints, 1979.

Warde, Anton. "Goethe, Schiller, Faust, and the Ideal: The Genesis of Irony in Faust." *The German Quarterly*, vol. 48, no. 2, Mar. 1975, pp. 175-186. www.jstor.org/stable/404438. 11 January 2019.

Weigand, Paul. "Schiller's Dramas as Opera Texts." *Monatshefte*, vol. 46, no. 5 Oct., 1954, pp. 249-259. *JSTOR*, www.jstor.org/stable/30166068. 15 June 2018.

Willson, Flora. "Of Time and the City: Verdi's *Don Carlos* and Its Parisian Critics." *19th-Century Music*, vol. 37, no. 3 (Spring 2014), pp. 188-210. 27 November 2018.

Zeck, John. "Composer's Datebook." *Your Classical*. www.yourclassical.org/programs/composers-datebook/episodes/2018/10/09. 17 March 2019.

INDEX

A

Alba, Duke of 4, 9, 11, 14, 26, 27, 29-30, 36-37, 38, 44-45, 47, 63, 66
d'Albret, Jeanne, Queen of Navarre 38-39
Alcalá, Don Diego de 7, 36
Alcalá, University of 7, 35
Alfieri, Count Vittorio 19
  Filippo II 19
Anne, Archduchess of Austria 8
Aristotle 79
d'Armagnac, Georges Cardinal 38-39
d'Aubigné, Agrippa 26-27, 48

B

Bedmar, Marquis of 40, 41
Bizet, Georges 101
Boileau, Nicolas 21
Boito, Arrigo 85
Brantôme, Pierre de 25, 31, 48
  Memoirs 25

C

Cabrera de Córdoba, Luis 17, 27, 48
  Historia de Felipe I, Rey de España 17
Cammarano, Salvatore 83
Campiston, Jean-Galbert de 19
  Andronic 19
Carlos, Don, Infante of Spain ix-xi, 2, 5-9, 11-14, 15-18, 22, 25, 26, 27-38, 44-50, 55-60, 62-70, 71-78, 86, 87-89, 94-100, 103, 104, 110-113, 114, 117-119
Castiglione, Baldassare 2
  Courtier, The 2
Cateau-Cambrésis, Treaty of 31
Catherine, Queen of Portugal 12
Catholic League 24
Charles V, Holy Roman Emperor (1519-1556) 1, 3-4, 7, 9, 25, 34, 35, 36, 44, 63, 69, 96, 98-99
Chénier, Marie-Joseph 20
  Philippe II 20
Chronos 31, 76
Cormon, Eugène 20
  Philippe II, roi d'Espagne, drame en cinq actes imité de Schiller, et précédé de l'Étudiant d'Alcalá prologue 20
Costa, Sir Michael 102
Council of Troubles ("Council of Blood") 14
Cura, José 118-119

D

Descartes, René 21
  Les passions de l'âme, 21
Dietrichstein, Adam von 6
Doria, Andrea 42
du Locle, Camille 84, 98-99, 100, 111

E

Eboli, Prince Ruy Gómez de 4, 5, 8-9, 11, 13, 26, 36, 44-45, 47, 61
Eboli, Princess 26, 44, 55, 61, 88, 89, 94-97

Egmont, Count Lamoral 4, 5, 8-9, 10, 14, 35-36, 56, 71
Enciso, Diego Jiménez de 25, 49
   El Príncipe Don Carlos 49
Erasmus of Rotterdam 3
Escorial Palace 13, 26
Espinosa, Cardinal 13
Eugénie, Empress of France 101

F

Ferdinand II, King of Aragon (1475-1516) 6
Fiesco, Gianluigi 42
Fourquevaux, Baron de 13
French Revolution (1789) 79

G

Gachard, Louis Prosper 18, 84-85
   Don Carlos et Philippe II 84-85
Ginés Pérez de Hita 25-26
Goethe, Johann Wolfgang von 51, 52
   Sorrows of Young Werther, The 52
Grand Inquisitor (character) 86, 91, 92-93, 102, 103
Granvelle, Cardinal de 10

H

Harnoncourt, Nikolaus 110
Henry II, King of France (1547-1559) 31, 61
Henry IV, King of France (1589-1610) 5, 24, 27, 38, 39, 40
Horace 78
Horn, Count of 14
Hugo, Victor 83

I

Inquisition, Spanish 10, 26, 35, 47, 55, 73, 74, 75-76, 78, 102-103
Isabella, Queen of Castile (1474-1504) 6

J

John of Austria, (Dom Juan) 9, 11, 35, 44
Jordan, Philippe 116-117
Juana, Princess of Spain 4, 7

K

Kant, Immanuel 59
   Critique of Judgment 59
Karl Eugen, Duke of Württemberg 51-52
Kaufmann, Josef 117-118, 120
Khan, Kamal 116
Klinger, Friedrich 52
   Sturm und Drang 52
Konwitschny, Peter 104

L

La Fayette, Madame 20, 21, 24, 25, 26, 29-30
   La Princesse de Clèves 21, 29-30
   La Princesse de Montpensier 20
   Zayde, 25
La Fontaine, Jean de 21
La Rochefoucauld, François, Duc de 42
Lauzière, Achille de 84, 101-102, 111
Le Noble, Eustache 42
Lebois, André 49-50
   Don Carlos, nouvelle historique 49-50
Lessing, Gotthold 52, 78
   Hamburgische Dramaturgie, 52
   Nathan der Weise, 78
Lope de Vega (Lope de Vega Carpio) 25
Louis XIV, King of France (1643-1715) 22, 28, 43

M

Machiavelli, Niccolò 40
   The Prince 40
Maffei, Count Andrea 83, 98

Man, John 15
Margaret of Parma, Regent of the Netherlands 9-10, 14
María of Portugal (Queen of Spain) 5, 12
Maria, Princess of Spain 4
Mary I, Queen of England (Mary Tudor) 5
Matthieu, Pierre 17, 48
Histoire de France, 17
Maximilian II, Holy Roman Emperor 8
McVicar, Sir David 110
Medici, Catherine de 5, 6, 12
Ménage, Gilles 21
Méry, Joseph 84, 111
Molière (Jean-Baptiste Poquelin) 21
Montalbán, Juan Pérez de 25
Montigny, Baron de 10, 45
Mozart, Wolfgang Amadeus 110
Don Giovanni 110

N

Napoleon III, Emperor of France 84, 101
Nero, Emperor of Rome 74
Nuitter (Charles Truinet) 103

O

Orange, William of (Prince of the Netherlands) 5, 10, 14, 16-17
Otway, Thomas 19, 20
Don Carlos, Prince of Spain 19

P

Paul V, Pope 40
Pérez, Antonio 13, 45, 48
Pérez, Gonzalo 2
Perrin, Émile 84
Philip II, King of Spain (1556-1598) ix-xi, 1-2, 2-4, 5-6, 8-18, 24, 25, 27, 28-35, 44-48, 53-54, 55-56, 57-60, 62-63, 64-66, 67-70, 71-78, 87-88, 89-90, 91, 92-93, 94-98, 103, 104
Piave, Francesco Maria 90
Posa, Marquis of (character) 36-37, 51, 53-54, 56-57, 57-58, 61-63, 64, 71-78, 86, 90, 94-100, 103, 104, 112-113
Puccini, Giacomo 110
Tosca 110

R

Racine, Jean 21
Bajazet 24
Bérénice 24
Retz, Cardinal de (Jean François Paul de Gondi) 42-43
La conjuration du comte de Fiesque 42
Mémoires 42
Ricordi, Giulio 85, 103
Rousseau, Jean-Jacques 51, 58
Royer, Alphonse 84

S

Saint-Évremond, Charles 42
Saint-Réal, César de x, 18, 19-50, 51, 53, 56, 60, 63, 70, 82, 84, 87, 89, 96, 97, 101, 104-107, 114, 121, 123-124
Conjuration des espagnols contre la république de Venise 25, 39-40
De l'usage de l'histoire 22
Dom Carlos, nouvelle historique x, 19-50, 51
Réconciliation du mérite avec de la fortune 22
Histoire de la conjuration des Gracques (attr.) 42
Saint-Sulpice, Everard de 39
Sallust 42
The Conspiracy of Catiline 42
San Yuste Monastery 26, 35, 96, 98

Sarrazin, Jean François (Sarasin) 42
La Conjuration de Valstein 42
Schiller, Friedrich x, 18, 19, 20, 28, 31, 32, 37, 42-43, 45, 47, 49, 51-80, 82-83, 88, 89, 90, 91-92, 92-93, 96, 98, 100, 101, 104, 105-107, 121, 123-124
 Die Jungfrau von Orleans 83
 Die Räuber 51-52, 52-53
 Die Verschwörung des Fiesco zu Genua 42-43, 52
 Don Karlos, Infant von Spanien x, 19, 20, 43, 49, 51-80, 82-83, 85-86, 87
 Kabale und Liebe, 53, 83
 Maria Stuart 80
 On Naïve and Sentimental Poetry 55
 On the Aesthetic Education of Man in a Series of Letters 59
 Wallenstein (trilogy) 80
Scribe, Eugène 84
Shakespeare, William 51, 83, 84
 King Lear 84
 Macbeth 84
 Otello 84, 91
Solera, Temistocle 83
Spanish Black Legend 15, 16, 28
St. Etienne, Abbé 39
Stuart, Henry (Lord Darnley) 6
Stuart, Mary (Mary Queen of Scots) 6

T
Teutsche Merkur, Der 54, 78
Thalia (literary journal) 53
Thou, Jacques Auguste de 17, 26-27, 38
 Historia sui temporis 17, 38, 48
Turquet de Mayerne, Louis 17, 26-27, 48
 Histoire Générale d'Espagne 17

V
Vaëz, Gabriel 84
Valois, Elisabeth de, Queen of Spain, xi, 5, 6, 11-12, 13, 16, 24, 25, 27-28, 29-39, 44-50, 55-64, 87-89, 94-98, 104, 112-113
Valois, Marguerite de 5
Vargas, Ramón 120-121, 121-123
Varillas, Antoine 21
Verdi, Giuseppe x, 18, 20, 28, 32, 35, 37, 45, 47, 49-50, 70, 81-107, 111, 116, 121-123
 Don Carlos (*Don Carlo*) x, 20, 45, 49-50, 81-107, 111, 116-117, 118-124
 Giovanna d'Arco 83
 Ernani 83
 Falstaff 83
 Inno delle nazioni 85
 Lombardi alla Prima Crociata, I (*Jérusalem*) 83, 84
 Luisa Miller 83-84, 91-92
 Macbeth 83
 Masnadieri, I 83
 Otello 83
Verhaeren, Emile 20
 Philippe II 20
Vesalius, Andreas 7, 36
Villedieu, Madame de 21, 24, 25, 26
 Annales galantes 21
 Galanteries grenadines, 25

W
Wagner, Richard 101, 110
Warlikowski, Krzystof 104, 117-118

X
Ximénès, Augustin-Louis, marquis de 19
 Dom Carlos 19
Ximénez de Enciso, Don Diego ix
 El Principe Don Carlos ix

www.ingramcontent.com/pod-product-compliance
Lightning Source LLC
Chambersburg PA
CBHW071849230426
43671CB00012B/2116